# Ramaphosa

RAY HARTLEY

# Ramaphosa

## Path to power

HURST & COMPANY, LONDON

First published in 2018 by Jonathan Ball Publishers, South Africa

First published in the United Kingdom in 2018 by
C. Hurst & Co. (Publishers) Ltd.,
41 Great Russell Street, London, WC1B 3PL
© Ray Hartley, 2018
All rights reserved.
Printed in the United Kingdom by Bell & Bain Ltd, Glasgow

Distributed in the United States, Canada and Latin America by
Oxford University Press, 198 Madison Avenue, New York, NY 10016,
United States of America.

A Cataloguing-in-Publication data record for this book
is available from the British Library.

ISBN: 978-1-78738-015-8


www.hurstpublishers.com

*To Zoë,*
*bringer of hope, light and life*

# Contents

# List of abbreviations

Amcu    Association of Mineworkers and Construction Union
ANC     African National Congress
AsgiSA   Accelerated and Shared Growth Initiative for South Africa
Azactu   Azanian Confederation of Trade Unions
Codesa   Convention for a Democratic South Africa
Cosatu   Congress of South African Trade Unions
Cusa    Council of Unions of South Africa
DA      Democratic Alliance
EFF     Economic Freedom Fighters
Fosatu    Federation of South African Trade Unions
Gear     Growth, Employment and Redistribution
HCI     Hosken Consolidated Investments
Mawu    Metal and Allied Workers Union
Nail     New Africa Investments Limited
NEC     national executive committee
Nedlac   National Economic Development and Labour Council
NP      National Party
NPA     National Prosecuting Authority
NUM    National Union of Mineworkers
Numsa   National Union of Metalworkers of South Africa
Nusas    National Union of South African Students
NWC    national working committee
PAC     Pan Africanist Congress
RDP     Reconstruction and Development Programme
SAA     South African Airways
SACP    South African Communist Party
Sactu    South African Congress of Trade Unions
Saftu    South African Federation of Trade Unions

| | |
|---|---|
| Sanco | South African National Civic Organisation |
| SAPS | South African Police Service |
| SARS | South African Revenue Service |
| Saso | South African Students' Organisation |
| SCM | Student Christian Movement |
| UDF | United Democratic Front |

# Introduction

*Suddenly, Ramaphosa was grinning. But just as quickly the smile disappeared and he was touching my sleeve conspiratorially: 'I am an enigma, you know.' – Anthony Butler*

Cyril Ramaphosa raised his right hand and took the oath of office as president of South Africa on 15 February 2018, two months after he narrowly won office as president of the ruling ANC.

To most South Africans, Ramaphosa represented an opportunity to reverse the nation's slide under Jacob Zuma. He pledged himself to a restoration of clean governance, a return to the rule of law and a faster pace of economic growth that would finally address the country's youth unemployment disaster.

Ramaphosa had taken power, but he remained an enigma. His first Cabinet was both a sweeping change and more of the same. He removed a swathe of Zuma's lackeys and took firm control of the financial heart of government but inexplicably retained other Zuma loyalists, even some who were universally regarded as incompetent. He retained the weak and impotent head of public prosecutions who had protected Zuma until the eleventh hour, but he acted decisively against the tax boss associated with Zuma.

The questions were many. What did Ramaphosa stand for? What motivated him? How would he govern? What were his real priorities?

It is not my objective to provide a comprehensive account of Ramaphosa's life. This has, in any event, been done by Anthony Butler in his admirable biography, *Cyril Ramaphosa*. Nor do I make any claim to illuminating the deep psychological motives that may or may not shape Ramaphosa's public persona, or that of others in the political limelight, intriguing though such a work might be.

Instead, I plan to stick to my knitting – the cut and thrust of politics, the great game that shapes the fortunes and destinies of nations. This is what interests me, and this is the craft that I have spent my working life refining as a journalist observing the unfolding of the great South African political spectacle. From the dying kicks of apartheid to the birth of the new democratic order and the emergence of new maladies, many of which were not anticipated, South Africa's political story has been compelling. So much is at stake.

It was once a simpler story, in which the demons of apartheid fought to the death with the angels of the anti-apartheid struggle. But it has evolved into something far more complex and difficult, although the old pattern persists of seeing its players as either demons or angels.

In the amusing preface to his biography, Butler recounts the game of cat-and-mouse he played to get Ramaphosa's coope-ration during a meeting at his Sandton offices: 'Suddenly Rama-phosa was grinning. But just as quickly the smile disappeared and he was touching my sleeve conspiratorially: "I am an enigma, you know."'[1] I first encountered Ramaphosa when I served as the minutes secretary of Working Group Two in the Convention for a Democratic South Africa (Codesa) negotiations over the shape of a post-apartheid South Africa. Ramaphosa served on that com-mittee, and it is no exaggeration to say that the sheer force of his personality and his tactical nous drove those negotiations to their successful conclusion.

If there is one thing that has defined Ramaphosa's political life, it is the description 'negotiator'. Success in negotiations requires charm and charisma, but it also requires a ruthless eye for the opponent's weaknesses and an ability to strike a deal at a moment when you have reduced those sitting across the table to a state where they will accept the compromise that you offer on your terms.

Ramaphosa would become the lead negotiator for the African National Congress (ANC), the country's largest and most influential liberation movement, at talks over the end of apartheid and the writing of a new constitution. He would demonstrate his negotiating prowess by cowing the ANC's main opponent, the National Party (NP), which had ruled the country for over 40 years, into agreeing to free, unqualified elections for a fully democratic state that would be governed by a progressive constitution. This was not the accomplishment of an accommodator so much as the product of Ramaphosa's negotiating prowess. He got the turkeys to vote for Christmas.

But once the ink had dried on the Interim Constitution and Nelson Mandela was set to become South Africa's first democratically elected president, Ramaphosa found himself politically sidelined. The ANC chose his rival, Thabo Mbeki, to be Mandela's successor. Ramaphosa, who cut his teeth in the trade union movement and the mass internal struggle against apartheid, came from a tradition of robust and open democratic practice. Trade union congresses were held in public and there were sometimes raucous contestations for leadership roles. Mbeki came from the exile tradition where operations were clandestine and information was shared on a 'need-to-know' basis. Leadership decisions were taken behind closed doors and complete unity presented to the outside world.

Mbeki's presidency and that of his successor, Jacob Zuma, saw the application of this exile mindset to national politics, and the opacity of the ANC sat uneasily with the transparency, account-ability and openness of the Constitution of the republic.

The question everyone was asking as Ramaphosa took office in the Union Buildings was this: can the man in the middle lead from the front? In other words, can Ramaphosa disrupt the political narrative, transforming it from one of fear and rumour into one of hope and optimism? Can Ramaphosa drag the ANC out of the shadows and turn it into a modern political force that operates comfortably in a constitutional democracy?

This book attempts to answer these questions by looking at how Ramaphosa has handled the key challenges he has faced in the trade union movement, in business and in politics. These questions are not easy to answer because Ramaphosa remains one of the best-kept secrets in South African politics, seldom offering anything of himself beyond carefully considered public statements.

One of those I spoke to before writing this book was former mining executive Bobby Godsell. As a young man, Godsell sat opposite Ramaphosa during negotiations over wages and working conditions on Anglo American mines. He worked with Ramaphosa on the National Peace Accord, and encountered him again when Anglo entered into the first big empowerment deal of the democratic era, the sale of Johnnic to a consortium of black investors led by Ramaphosa. 'Remember,' Godsell told me, 'he's a man of many parts.' Ramaphosa came from a middle-class background – his father was a policeman. And then he had studied law. 'Law and politics are often pretty connected,' remarked Godsell.

Ramaphosa is a fascinating subject because he spans so many of the territories where this story has unfolded. He was a student leader. He was critically involved in the struggle against apartheid as a trade unionist. And then he became the key figure at the constitutional talks to shape the new democratic order. He exited formal politics to build a business empire, and then returned to the political coalface only to find that the machinery he had helped put in place was badly in need of repair. Of course, the fact that he has now become president of the republic makes him all the more intriguing a subject.

He is at once charming and reserved. He defers to authority and yet he projects authority. He is driven to navigate the country's destiny and yet, at times, appears helplessly afloat on the tide. What does he stand for? The answer is at once in plain sight and obscured by clouds of circuitous reasoning.

*

Let us start where all political narratives should, with the greater context. This is the age of disruption. Wherever you care to look, you will see traditional political paradigms collapsing and a new raw politics emerging. Propelling this is a rising tide of anger at the failure of the establishment – as often a settled democratic order as an authoritarian one – to deliver answers to a set of core problems that are the result of the way the world of work is changing. Rationalisation, outsourcing and vast increases in productivity have been followed by the appearance of machines and algorithms that can do the tasks that once employed millions and fed their families. Economic certainties about the ability of democratic capitalism to deliver a rising level of prosperity for the ordinary person have been smashed by a succession of financial crises and by the fact that the wealth effect has not benefited the vast majority of people.

At the same time, the capacity of a society to insulate itself from these effects, or from the social or economic collapse of other states, has lessened as the world has become more integrated. In the US, Donald Trump took office – somewhat disingenuously – as a man of the people who wished to overturn the political apple-cart. What got him elected was that he could credibly argue that he was not part of the government that had presided over two decades of wealth accumulation without the benefits being spread to ordinary people. In the UK, a similar revolt against the old ways of doing things by those on the receiving end of failed economic policies saw, first, a vote in favour of leaving the European Union – the so-called Brexit vote – and, second, a surprising electoral swing against Conservative prime minister Theresa May and towards Labour leader Jeremy Corbyn, until then regarded as unelectable. In France, the traditional parties were swept aside by Emmanuel Macron's En Marche! movement. Long before these disruptions, across North Africa, the Arab Spring had come and gone. Governments that had been entrenched for decades were toppled and turmoil was now raging over the next generation of leadership. This global tide of disillusionment with the established order also found its way to South Africa, where the problems are, if anything, starker.

South Africa, though blighted by colonialism and then by apartheid, has had a more hopeful recent history than many other nations. In 1994, Nelson Mandela became the country's first democratic president, promising to heal the country's wounds and usher in a new age of prosperity. Mandela has been buried, his successor, Thabo Mbeki, has become a bitter observer of the decline in government performance, and Jacob Zuma became mired in a succession of scandals that would have brought most leaders to their knees in a functional democracy.

The South Africa that Ramaphosa seeks to lead is no longer the Rainbow Nation of Mandela. A trend towards corruption and cronyism, which began not long after the advent of the democratic era, was rapidly accelerated during Zuma's nine years in office.

The Gupta family, which had close business ties with Zuma via his relatives, inserted its cronies into government departments and state-owned enterprises, and milked public-sector infrastructure contracts for billions in a brazen act of 'state capture', the term used to describe the funnelling of state resources into private hands under Zuma's watch.

Those parts of the post-apartheid media that survived politically connected takeovers were subject to constant threats of regulation by state tribunals and accused of attempting to bring about 'regime change' when they exposed graft and corruption.

There remained a vigorously independent section of the media that took on the role of publicly exposing the capture of the state. The judiciary remained independent, although the best judges in the world are mere ornaments if cases of graft are not brought before them. In civil society, veterans of the ruling ANC and activist NGOs loudly called for an end to state capture.

The official opposition party, the Democratic Alliance (DA), has attempted to pivot from being a party of the elite (with its former racial connotations lingering on) to one that could seriously challenge for power by winning the confidence of black voters, but has stumbled through its own crisis. Its leadership, struggling to reconcile a past of post-colonial smugness with a future as a party of transformation and economic growth, is convincing more and more voters but is a very long way away from being able to command a majority.

It would seem from this description that South Africa is fast becoming the 'basket case' that observers on the right have always believed it would. But this is not yet the case. Zuma may have gone a long way towards ruining the country's democratic institutions, but they are still very much alive. The ANC itself showed it was aware of the danger of Zuma's toxic state-capture project when it voted against his preferred successor and in favour of Ramaphosa at its December 2017 conference.

Zuma ignited the fire of rebellion when he tried to cut the party out of executive decision-making in favour of his circle of cronies and corrupt business associates. By the winter of 2017, Jacob Zuma's presidency was entering its eighth year amid its biggest controversy – his firing of the Finance minister, Pravin Gordhan, a critic of state capture. Zuma's familial relationship with the Gupta family had been widely criticised, most prominently by the Public Protector, Thuli Madonsela, who had called for a judicial inquiry into the scandal.

But Gordhan was more than just a victim of Zuma's executive prejudices. He was the canary in the ANC's coal mine. Zuma had for some time wanted to get rid of him, but had balked when it became apparent that this would not enjoy the support of large sections of the ruling party. Gordhan's dismissal sent a signal to those in the ANC who were against Zuma but had accommodated him in the interests of projecting party unity. The signal was that it was time to step out of the shadows and take a stand. The fight for the soul of the ANC was under way.

After biding his time – perhaps for too long – Ramaphosa finally stepped up to lead the battle against state capture. To some he was a reluctant and opportunistic participant in the campaign. To others, Ramaphosa was studiously following the only path to power within the ANC, which has always viewed criticism as an assault by the 'enemy'. What is important is that the context in which Ramaphosa has returned to politics is fraught.

The fight against Zuma and his business cronies was a rebellion against corruption and the capturing of the state, but it also had an important ideological dimension. To understand this, it is necessary to go back to Zuma's rise to power in September 2007. At the ANC's Polokwane conference, Zuma overcame impossible odds to unseat Thabo Mbeki as party president. Mbeki had been accused of being 'aloof' and of failing to consult the party as he centralised decision-making in the executive. But cutting through the rejection of Mbeki was another dynamic. In 1996, Mbeki was the moving force behind the Growth, Employment and Redistribution (Gear) policy, a centrist macroeconomic platform that sought to place government finances on a sound footing by controlling expenditure, reducing the deficit and encouraging growth led by private-sector investment. Gear was the successor to the left-of-centre Reconstruction and Development Programme (RDP), which had been introduced by Nelson Mandela in 1994. The RDP envisioned the state as a more active agent in redistribution.

One of the reasons Zuma was able to dislodge Mbeki was that he promised an end to Gear's conservative macroeconomic programme and a return to a more interventionist state. This sat well with the party's left wing and its allies in the trade union movement and the South African Communist Party (SACP), who endorsed his campaign with gusto. The then head of the Congress of South African Trade Unions (Cosatu), Zwelinzima Vavi, famously proclaimed that opposing Zuma's campaign for the presidency was like 'trying to fight against the big wave of the tsunami'.[2]

In reality, Mbeki had already begun to change gears, as it were, adopting a new programme, the Accelerated and Shared Growth Initiative for South Africa (AsgiSA), which sought to fire up the economy by bolstering infrastructure spending. Having failed to consult the party thoroughly when he dropped the RDP in favour of Gear, he attempted to make up for this by consulting thoroughly on the introduction of AsgiSA. But it was too little, too late for the left, which saw Zuma as more likely to implement their more interventionist agenda. Of course, once Zuma was in power he shed these erstwhile allies one by one as he demonstrated that he was, if anything, more of a nationalist and a capitalist than Mbeki.

Exactly where Ramaphosa stood on this ideological continuum between the centrist fiscal discipline of Mbeki and the aggressive capitalist nationalism of Zuma was not immediately obvious when he returned to politics. But the outlines of a 'Ramaphosa way' began to emerge as he waded deeper and deeper into the battle.

Ramaphosa won by a narrow margin, and his first actions in office showed that he was determined to turn the ship around. It was telling that he returned Nhlanhla Nene – fired by Zuma – to the Finance ministry and appointed Pravin Gordhan – another Zuma casualty – to head the Public Enterprises ministry. He was taking control of the financial levers with a view to returning the country to fiscal stability. He was closing the taps on the state capture enterprise, removing its ability to dispense patronage.

*

More than two decades of democracy have failed to deliver a significant change in the lives of many who were supposed to be liberated after 1994. It is not true, as some assert, that for most people life under democracy is worse than under apartheid. More people than ever enjoy the benefits of piped water, electricity, housing, access to education and, vitally, access to the largest social welfare net in the developing world. But South Africa has manifestly failed to reach its full potential. The proportion of those unemployed, as a percentage of adults who might have jobs, is shockingly high, and the social welfare net does little more than file off the rough edges of poverty.

The single greatest achievement of post-apartheid South Africa has been the establishment of a large new middle class, which has benefited from affirmative action, black economic empowerment and growing civil service employment. By some reckonings, as many as 10 million black people entered the middle class in the roughly twenty years after the end of apartheid.[3] But this middle class lives a precarious and highly indebted existence that is threatened by the state's diminishing access to revenue. While advancement in the job market has benefited the middle class, the youth have struggled to find a place in the new establishment. A failing education system and an economy that continues to shed jobs has led to a rise in youth unemployment. The middle class finds itself increasingly having to fund education, health and security privately, while new taxes, such as the much-hated e-toll system on Gauteng's roads, have caused them to turn on the establishment.

The rising tide of graft and cronyism has contributed to this rebellion in two ways: it has reduced the state's ability to deliver services, and it has removed opportunities for advancement and entrepreneurship from all but a small sliver of politically connected people. The ruling ANC, once regarded as politically unassailable, has begun to take on water, suffering electoral losses in key metropoles such as Tshwane and Nelson Mandela Bay, having already lost the elements of the black middle class it once relied on in the coloured community in the Western Cape and among many Indian South Africans. The party's response has been to circle the wagons and promise more 'radical economic transformation', a policy that will further cement the defection of the black middle class, which now has assets and desires economic stability.

Ramaphosa is acutely aware that the ANC needs to demonstrate an improvement in the lives of ordinary people if it is to win back its lost support in the metropolitan areas.

The stage has been set for someone to grasp the nettle and lead the country out of this crisis. Into this fractured and disrupted political context steps our protagonist, Cyril Ramaphosa.

# ONE

## *Consciousness*

When I was in detention, I came to realise that friends
are like teabags. You boil the water. And you use them once.
*– Cyril Ramaphosa*

Matamela Cyril Ramaphosa was born on 17 November 1952 in
Johannesburg. It was a momentous year for South African politics.
The ANC – then still legal – would launch its Defiance Campaign,
the first major national mass resistance campaign against apartheid. The National Party had been in power for just over four years,
and centuries of racial discrimination were now being codified in
legislation that unashamedly handed whites control over every
aspect of black lives. Among apartheid's many humiliations was
the requirement that blacks carry passes in the urban areas; the
public burning of these passbooks would be a key feature of the
campaign. It was also the 300th anniversary of the arrival of
Dutch official Jan van Riebeeck at the Cape, signifying the start
of colonial rule.

Ramaphosa began his schooling in the Western Native Township,
near Johannesburg. When he was just ten years old, his family was
moved from that township to Soweto, where he attended Tshilidzi
Primary School in Chiawelo. He completed his schooling at Sibasa
in Venda in 1971.

The young Ramaphosa had already demonstrated a defiant

attitude towards apartheid. Anthony Butler records how Ramaphosa responded to the deferential treatment accorded to whites
during a school event at Mukumbai, the chief's kraal in Sibasa:
'The senior police officer present, Captain Madzena, treated the
whites with the then customary exaggerated deference. He gave
priority to their needs and accommodated their wishes, leading
them to the front of the crowd. Such favours would have been
accepted by them and others present as quite natural.

'Cyril, however, emerged visibly upset from the crowd and began
to complain eloquently that this was the chiefs' place. "Why", he
asked, "must whites be given preference over Africans, even here,
at the expense of the true owners of the place?"'[1]

\*

Cyril Ramaphosa's politics were forged during the 1970s in the
furnace of the struggle against apartheid. When most South Africans think of the struggle, they recall the Soweto uprising of 1976
as its seminal moment. There were, in fact, many aspects of the
1970s that made it a decade distinct from the decade of open mass
mobilisation that was the 1980s.

The ANC had been severely damaged by the apartheid state in
the 1960s; with its leadership imprisoned on Robben Island and its
organisational machinery in exile, the party had a very low profile
within the country. If black South Africans looked to a leader, they
were as likely to choose Stephen (Steve) Bantu Biko as they were
to choose Nelson Mandela or the ANC's exiled leader, OR Tambo.

Biko was the leading figure in the Black Consciousness Movement. As a student, he had been a member of the National Union
of South African Students (Nusas), which had adopted an anti-
apartheid stance but which relied on the support of the mostly
white student population. When Biko attended a student conference at Rhodes University in Grahamstown in July 1967,[2] he

was informed that the white and Indian students would sleep in dormitories while black students were expected to sleep in a church. Biko and others walked out of Nusas and decided that, rather than be part of so-called non-racial movements, blacks needed to organise on their own and develop a consciousness of their social programme that was not affected by the interventions of other more privileged races. This was the basis of the Black Consciousness philosophy. Biko would define Black Consciousness as follows:

> Black Consciousness is in essence the realisation by the black man of the need to rally together with his brothers around the cause of their oppression – the blackness of their skin – and to operate as a group in order to rid themselves of the shackles that bind them to perpetual servitude. It seeks to demonstrate the lie that black is an aberration from the 'normal' which is white. It is a manifestation of a new realization that by seeking to run away from themselves and to emulate the white man, blacks are insulting the intelligence of whoever created them black. Black Consciousness, therefore takes cognizance of the deliberateness of God's plan in creating black people black.[3]

He went on to say that Black Consciousness 'seeks to infuse the black community with a new-found pride in themselves, their efforts, their value systems, their culture, their religion and their outlook to life . . . Blacks are out to completely transform the system and to make of it what they wish. Such a major undertaking can only be realized in an atmosphere where people are convinced of the truth inherent in their stand. Liberation therefore is of paramount importance in the concept of Black Consciousness, for we cannot be conscious of ourselves and yet remain in bondage. We want to attain the envisioned self which is a free self.'[4]

Biko and his fellow activists formed the South African Students'

Organisation (Saso), which was launched at the University of the North – an institution designated for black learners.

\*

In 1972, Cyril Ramaphosa began his studies at the University of the North, known as 'Turfloop'. His political development would unfold in an environment similar to that which had inspired Biko. As Butler writes, Turfloop and other 'black' universities drew students from relatively financially stable households, and graduates were expected to become cooperative members of the homeland civil service or the parts of the apartheid state that required black administrators: 'Racial domination was evident in every aspect of the students' lives outside the university, and it was reproduced within it too. The universities were dominated by an Afrikaner bureaucracy at the level of the rectorate, the council and senate. The academic staff, especially at senior levels, was overwhelmingly white.'[5]

While at university, Ramaphosa became involved with the Student Christian Movement (SCM) and immediately began to transform it into an activist organisation. He and a young Frank Chikane – who would go on to head the South African Council of Churches before becoming Director General in the Presidency under Thabo Mbeki – saw to it that the SCM was restructured and that a new constitution was developed. Butler observes: 'He produced a new constitution, and his fellow members were obliged to debate its contents endlessly. In this constitution, Cyril inserted a "doctrinal basis" section that explicitly repudiated racism and the unjust system of apartheid. Cyril's trademark success in creating a new institution was based on careful drafting of the constitution, careful strategic planning, and relentless persuasiveness in public and private meetings.'[6]

When the apartheid state cracked down on Saso in 1974, the

SCM stepped into the breach on the Turfloop campus and Ramaphosa moved to the front of the political firing line. The apartheid
state paid lip service to legal formality, but it was a de facto police
state, capable of severe repression and even political killings.
Enemies were identified and subjected to brutal treatment. In
Ramaphosa's case, he was held in solitary confinement in Pretoria Central Prison for 11 months. Solitary confinement was a
savage extra-legal punishment meted out to those on whom the
police did not have sufficient evidence to convict in court. Frances
Baard, a trade union organiser from Kimberley jailed in 1960,
described her experience of solitary confinement:

> I wouldn't wish for anybody to spend a whole year in solitary
> confinement. Really, it is a terrible thing. You sit and think.
> Walk to the window. The window was right up; I had to stand
> on something – the toilet was next to the window – so I could
> stand on the toilet to see a little hole there at the window. And
> you still don't see anything because the cell was downstairs,
> underground. You stay there in that cell, sit for a while, and
> then walk for a while. It was quite a big cell. Then I sit again.
> Sometimes I would sing some songs. You talk to yourself but
> you don't know what to say! You hear people talking outside but
> you can't even see them.[7]

Detention without trial could mean spending 'a whole year without anything to read and no one to talk to. And a light on in the
cell all the time. All day and at night too, the light on. You can't
sleep.'[8]

The most high-profile victim of this form of punishment was
Biko himself. In the wake of the Soweto uprising and growing
national ferment, Biko was arrested on 18 August 1977 outside
Grahamstown. He was detained in Port Elizabeth, where he was
subjected to brutal interrogation by security policemen. On 11 Sep-

tember, the gravely injured Biko was moved to Pretoria Central Prison, where he died on 12 September.[9]

Anthony Butler quotes Ramaphosa on his bleak period in detention: 'I never benefited from sitting down and having political discourse with fellow detainees and comrades. It is something I still feel I regret deeply. Those who were in a group with other people were able to strengthen each other, to have discussions on a whole variety of things, and I didn't have that opportunity because I was on my own.'[10] Ramaphosa did not talk about detention, except once when he said: 'When I was in detention, I came to realise that friends are like teabags. You boil the water. And you use them once.'[11]

Detention without trial was politically destabilising, too. Those whom the authorities did not charge were sometimes believed to have turned state witness against those on trial. Of course, such beliefs would be laid to rest once the trial began and the detained person did not appear as a witness, but by then a lot of damaging anxiety had been created.

The Black Consciousness poet Tshenuwani Farisani, described by Butler as 'a major influence on Cyril's political thought',[12] was a victim of brutality in detention. Farisani's story, although harrowing, was typical of the experience of many black South Africans. In 1951, when he was four years old, his family was uprooted from the fertile Songozi Tsapila area of Louis Trichardt without compensation. The family would be removed again in 1959 and in 1961. Farisani became an articulate voice for the oppressed, expressing the pain caused by apartheid in his writing. In 1996, he would tell the Truth and Reconciliation Commission of his harrowing experience while being held in detention: 'The four detentions . . . affected me as a person, affected my wife, my parents, my children, my sister, my relatives and my friends. And in this process friendships have been broken, family ties have been shattered and my father died without enjoying the freedom that I am enjoying today. He died with hope but he never lived to realise that hope.'[13]

Farisani recounted: 'I was made to do press-ups, to stand on my head, how can I stand on my top, you know I was very stout? They took me and made me stand on my head and then they kicked me. They boxed me as I was just like that. You know those people were very powerful. Imagine picking somebody like me, you know, they threw me up, throwing me down again on the cement, on concrete cement . . . You know there are scars here on my knees, the head was very swollen. I was given a cloth to take blood from the floor. I was made to use the cloth in wiping the blood from the face and even the body.'[14]

Ramaphosa had first met Farisani when he visited his school to address its debating society on the topic 'Knowledge is more important than money'.[15] In 1975, Farisani addressed the Black People's Convention, of which he was president: 'Blacks, courageous sons and daughters of Mother Africa, I commend you for your courage, for your determination and for your undaunted zeal to stand against all odds, natural and man-made, for the sake of your liberation and that of your country. POWER TO THE PEOPLE. POWER TO THE STRUGGLE. Persistence and fortitude are the pinnacles of a successful struggle. Azania shall be free and soon.'[16]

Ramaphosa's proximity to the Black Consciousness leadership resulted in a second period of detention under the Terrorism Act in 1976, following the Soweto student uprising. He was held for six months in Johannesburg Central Police Station, known until 1998 as John Vorster Square. The building had been named after John Vorster, the architect of South Africa's security legislation as Minister of Justice under Prime Minister Hendrik Verwoerd. By the time Ramaphosa was held in this notorious building – eight activists are known to have died while being held there – Vorster had been prime minister for ten years.

Once he had completed his studies at Turfloop, Ramaphosa became a clerk for a firm of Johannesburg attorneys, completing his BProc degree in 1981. By then he was already contemplating a career outside the law – in both senses.

. In September 1980, the Council of Unions of South Africa (Cusa) was formed, incorporating nine affiliated trade unions. The launch of the new federation was attended by a large number of Soweto politicians. A Soweto Civic Association spokesman said: 'Everybody in Soweto is a worker. Whatever the difference in our living standards, we have that in common.'[17] Ramaphosa was drawn to the Black Consciousness-leaning federation, where he became a legal adviser.

But, even as he began working for the union movement, the political ground was shifting under South Africans' feet. The ANC, whose role in sparking the 1976 uprising had been minimal, had nonetheless been its major beneficiary. Young people being hunted down by the apartheid police, or wanting to make a more serious contribution to the struggle, had crossed South Africa's borders in search of the exiled liberation movements. Once across the border, they found that the Africanist movements that could be said to be kin to Black Consciousness, such as the Pan Africanist Congress (PAC), were in disarray. By contrast, the ANC had offices, an infrastructure supported by sympathetic governments and a guerilla army in training. The ANC was soon recruiting a force of 'highly motivated and well-educated (in contrast to the recruits of the early 1960s) saboteurs', the historian Tom Lodge observes.[18]

The ANC began to make its presence felt inside the country, carrying out no fewer than 112 attacks and bombings between 1976 and 1981. Some of the targets had a high profile. Sasol's synthetic oil refineries, at Sasolburg and Secunda, were bombed in June 1980, power stations in the then Eastern Transvaal were hit in July 1981, and there were numerous attacks on police stations using grenades, rockets and bombs. The attacks were largely demonstrative, however, serving as a kind of 'armed propaganda'. Lodge comments: 'On the whole, their intention seems to have been to inspire confidence among the dominated population rather than terror within the white community.'[19]

While the guerilla campaign and associated acts of sabotage brought the ANC back into focus, the exiled movement began to act more and more like a government in waiting. In London, the movement's president, Oliver Tambo, attended his daughter's wedding in St Paul's Cathedral in 1981. The global establishment would soon succumb to the ANC's charm offensive, and impose financial and investment sanctions to squeeze sources of finance for the apartheid government.

On the ground, 'congress' was back, and a new generation of mass organisations emerged, preferring the apparent effectiveness of the ANC to the growing disorganisation of Black Consciousness. Cyril Ramaphosa took note. He would soon take a decision to shift the country's most powerful emerging union out of the Black Consciousness stable and into the ANC fold. But first, he would undertake the task of building an organisation where trade unionists had feared to tread – in the mine hostels and compounds.

## TWO

# *The man who sat across the table*

The Chamber is the elephant and we are the mosquito. The
mosquito will kill the elephant. – *James Motlatsi*

Following growing labour confrontation in the 1970s and the
popular uprising of 1976, the apartheid government set out to
bring order – and, in its view, control – to the labour relations environment. The Wiehahn Commission, established in the wake of
the landmark strikes in Natal in 1973, produced its report on the
way forward on 1 May 1979. Its recommendations were sweeping.
It proposed the legal recognition of black trade unions, the removal
of job reservation based on race, the introduction of a closed-shop
bargaining system and the establishment of an industrial court
to resolve legal disputes.

There was a quid pro quo, however. Black trade unions would
be required to register with the state, giving the government ultimate control over the very existence of a trade union as a legal
entity. The Wiehahn report was, nonetheless, a major victory for
organised labour, opening up the possibility of far wider unionisation. Attention began to focus on the biggest prize of all: the
750 000 unorganised mineworkers in the rich mineral belt in the
north of the country.

Mineworkers were among the most exploited workers in the

country. The political structure of South Africa had been designed around the need for young blacks to migrate to the Witwatersrand to seek work as miners. The absence of economic opportunities in the black homelands and in neighbouring states such as Lesotho, the lack of opportunity for land tenure and the vigorous work of mine recruiting agencies saw a steady flow of young men to the 'opportunity' presented by mining.

Once at the mines, the workers were barracked in cramped single-sex hostels, some of which had bed bases made of concrete. It is fair to say that they were regarded as less than human by the mine owners and by the state that allowed these conditions to exist.

South Africa's ore concentrates lie deep underground, and so miners spent their days working stopes in stiflingly hot temperatures. Accidents were frequent, sometimes resulting in the loss of limb or life. When I visited a mining operation some 3.5 km below the surface twenty years after the end of apartheid, it was a terrifying place. The sweat runs off your body in rivers in the cramped spaces where drills cleave the rock face. Improvements wrought by decades of unionism have made mining safer and better rewarded, but there is no escaping the fact that men have to be sent deep underground to retrieve gold-bearing ore under extreme circumstances.

Among those who immediately saw the opportunity presented by the Wiehahn reforms was Cyril Ramaphosa. In 1981, after he had completed his BProc degree through correspondence, he began working for Cusa,[1] which did not allow whites to occupy leadership positions. Until then, union organisers had found it impossible to penetrate the cordon of barbed wire and security fences that surrounded the mine hostels in order to meet with and organise workers.

Cusa's rival, the Federation of South African Trade Unions

(Fosatu), was also attempting to organise on the mines. The initiative was led by Bernie Fanaroff – in later life a distinguished radio astronomer – of the Metal and Allied Workers Union (Mawu), a Fosatu affiliate. He recalled how Mawu was shunted aside by Ramaphosa: 'We heard from workers . . . that when Bobby [Godsell, of Anglo American] heard that Mawu was organising the mines, he suddenly dropped his opposition to NUM [National Union of Mineworkers, established in 1982], so we couldn't get into the plants but the NUM could. I'm bad at getting together big groups of people . . . Cyril put together a big team and hit the ground with a lot of resources and access as well . . . I didn't like taking risks . . . and you needed to. He was a very good manager.'[2]

When Cusa decided to allocate a large portion of its meagre funds to organising mineworkers, the matter became political, with the exiled ANC being asked to intervene. The ANC refused to condemn the Cusa initiative. The assumption that the ANC would automatically go against the Black Consciousness union was proved wrong. Ramaphosa no doubt took note. How might he have reacted if the ANC had gone against Cusa? Would this have altered his political trajectory?

It took all of Ramaphosa's strategic and tactical instincts to start the National Union of Mineworkers (NUM). His approach was simple: find a crack in the massive edifice of the Anglo American Corporation that would allow organisation and then expand this beachhead into a permanent unionised zone.

The head of industrial relations at Anglo American was the enlightened Bobby Godsell, who was in favour of the unionisation of black workers. As Anthony Butler tells it, 'Ramaphosa identified a window of opportunity. He presented himself as a person of reason and moderation, who recognised that worker organisation could benefit both bosses and union members . . . Godsell was inclined to make life easy for NUM, readily conceding access to

Anglo mines and later agreeing to recognise the union even when its very small membership did not really justify this action. Cyril had managed to get the union's foot in the door. Anglo would never get it out again.'[3]

Michael Spicer, who was a senior executive at Anglo American at the time, told me Ramaphosa was a powerful adversary across the negotiating table: 'He's a very skilled negotiator. He knows how to read his opponents. He knows how to tactically retreat.' He understood how the balance of forces could be tilted with a simple manoeuvre.

The mine hostel compounds had been impenetrable fortresses where unions could not gain access. But once Ramaphosa had secured an agreement to permit organisation, the effect was to reverse this quite dramatically. The hostels were flipped; they became union strongholds and were soon no-go areas for management.

Under Ramaphosa, the NUM would become a highly effective union. It developed its research capacity and approached wage negotiations with an increasingly detailed understanding of company financials and where the weak points lay. Ramaphosa was capable of charm, but if provoked could project a cold, controlled anger that was a deterrent to challenging him on all but the most serious grounds. Butler recounts how, after an arduous round of negotiations in 1985, a mine general manager waved a copy of the agreement reached in front of Ramaphosa and said: 'Now you had better tell those members of yours to stick to this agreement.' Ramaphosa responded: 'Who the fuck do you think you are? You can't give me instructions. None of you can give me instructions. Don't you ever dare tell me what I have to do.'[4]

Ramaphosa realised that Godsell was the right negotiating partner for the union. They became comfortable enough with each other to develop informal ways of solving problems between the union and management. Godsell told me they would get together at the Koffiehuis restaurant in Johannesburg's Carlton Centre to explore potential 'zones of agreement' when formal discussions were faltering.

*

Ramaphosa's decision to align the NUM with the ANC and the internal mass movement played no small part in shifting the balance of forces during the later phases of the anti-apartheid struggle. Perhaps that 1982 decision by the ANC not to interfere in Cusa's attempt, through Ramaphosa, to establish a mineworkers' union paved the way.

Through the early 1980s, there had been several attempts to unify the union movement into a single federation. In 1983, the United Democratic Front (UDF) was launched at Rocklands, outside Cape Town. An alliance of community, civic, student and religious bodies, the UDF became the body that led the mass internal uprising against apartheid. Although it chose red, black and yellow as its colours, rather than the black, green and gold of the ANC, it was clearly an ANC-aligned formation and many of its leaders were clandestine members of the ANC. After the launch of the UDF, and as the tide of mass protest grew, seven unions – known as the 'magnificent seven' in struggle circles – opted to join the alliance.

Ramaphosa was ready to move out from under the Black Consciousness umbrella of Cusa. He and his fellow NUM leaders accordingly took the momentous decision to lead the NUM out of Cusa and into an alliance with the UDF. The effect was to swing the balance of forces within the union movement – the NUM was the country's largest union by 1985 – in favour of the 'ANC camp'. Ramaphosa had identified that his union's interests – and perhaps his own political ambitions – would best be served by switching horses to the ANC, which was the most effective anti-apartheid force, and which was, through the UDF and its growing international profile, winning the race to lead the liberation of South Africa.

Talk of a new national federation to unite all the country's major unions under one umbrella began to gather steam. Cusa and the Azanian Confederation of Trade Unions (Azactu), which shared its Black Consciousness outlook, rejected the idea of a new formation, but the NUM remained committed to exploring the possibility, along with several other major unions and Fosatu.

Ramaphosa was to become one of the driving forces behind the new federation. On 8 and 9 June 1985, he chaired unity talks at Ipeleng, in Soweto. He set out five principles: non-racialism; one union, one industry; worker control; representation based on paid-up membership; and cooperation at a national level.[5] The five points may or may not have been authored by Ramaphosa, but they bore the hallmarks of a savvy political intervention. They nodded to the ANC-aligned unions (non-racialism and the national character) and acknowledged the more worker-orientated unions (worker control and representation based on membership).

A series of unity meetings culminated in a meeting in November 1985 to launch the new federation. Some 760 delegates representing 33 unions gathered at Howard College, on the campus of the University of Natal, in Durban. Ramaphosa, by now entrenched as the driving force behind union unity, was the convener of the launch congress. His negotiating skills were once more necessary and he had to assert himself from the chair at times.

If Ramaphosa was the driving force, Cosatu's emerging leader was Jay Naidoo. Naidoo, the secretary general of the Sweet Food and Allied Workers Union, was an organiser for Fosatu, the largest of the union formations that would join the new federation. He would go on to become the new federation's first general secretary. He recalls: 'The air was thick with political tension and suspicion. I was very nervous. If elected to a leadership position I was going

27

to have to pull together disparate elements that seemed to be always at loggerheads with each other.'[6]

One of the sticking points was the launch date for the new federation, and when voices were raised over this, Ramaphosa said he would not chair a meeting where participants spoke aggressively to each other. Apologies followed and the date of 1 December was agreed on.[7] Naidoo says that 'Cyril was in pain and unwell that day, and I was aware of the stress he was under. He was our lynchpin, and if he was sick we were in trouble. But he soldiered on.'[8]

Previous unity talks had collapsed, but this time Ramaphosa and the other union leaders working on the talks pulled it off. Ramaphosa told the assembled delegates: 'The formation of this congress represents an enormous victory for the working class of this country . . . In the next few years we will be putting our heads together, not only to make sure we reach Pretoria, but also to make a better life for workers in the country. What we have to make clear is that a giant has arisen and will confront all that stands in its way.'[9]

It was a speech that committed the federation to the political struggle – to 'reach Pretoria' – while underlining the worker focus it would seek to maintain. Ramaphosa would handle negotiations to ensure that the new federation's leadership was spread evenly across the political spectrum of the affiliates. The name of the new federation – the Congress of South African Trade Unions – also nodded in the ANC direction, closely resembling that of the ANC-aligned South African Congress of Trade Unions (Sactu).

The arrival of a broadly ANC-aligned union federation would prove crucial in the years to come. While political organisations could be banned and prevented from meeting, the apartheid government had to consider the economic disruption that would result from taking such action against unions. Cosatu would suffer

Cyril Ramaphosa, with Alec Erwin in the background, at the
formation of Cosatu in Durban in 1985.
(Paul Weinberg/South Photographs/Africa Media Online)

its share of repression, but was always sufficiently intact to provide
the anti-apartheid mass democratic movement with a national
network when state repression hit union and UDF organisations
during successive states of emergency.

Jay Naidoo was elected as Cosatu's first general secretary and
Elijah Barayi as its president. Ramaphosa, along with Sydney
Mufamadi, Frank Chikane and Father Smangaliso Mkhatshwa,
formed a 'core committee' within the mass democratic movement
that communicated with the exiled ANC in Lusaka, Zambia, via
Mac Maharaj. In March 1986, a Cosatu delegation, including
Ramaphosa and Naidoo, travelled to Lusaka to meet with the
ANC president, Oliver Tambo. Also present were Chris Hani, Mac
Maharaj and Thabo Mbeki, whose political path would cross
Ramaphosa's dramatically in the following decade.

As a result of the visit to Lusaka, Ramaphosa became close to
Joe Slovo, general secretary of the South African Communist
Party (SACP) and the apartheid government's 'enemy number one'.
Slovo would one day support Ramaphosa's political rise within

29

the ANC. For now, they shared a political bond over worker militancy. A decade later, at Slovo's memorial service, Ramaphosa would recall that he and former NUM president James Motlatsi had first met Slovo 'in a hotel room in the mid-1980s':[10] 'He struck us as a complete contrast of what South Africans were fed by the NP government propaganda. He was a warm, jolly and robust bespectacled man with a good listening ear. The party had just published a pamphlet commemorating the 1946 mineworkers' strike. He wanted to know whether we would be agreeable to the distribution of some 2 000 copies of the pamphlet among the mineworkers. He was taken aback when we said we wanted 10 000 copies.'[11] Slovo, 'an efficient and effective revolutionary who could keep his word',[12] was Ramaphosa's introduction to the ANC left's inner circle. Mac Maharaj recalled: 'We never told the mass organisations what to do. Together we explored ideas then it was left to them to pursue what they considered best within the dynamics of the organisations they were serving.'[13]

Ramaphosa's relationship with the ANC was sealed when a modest, softly spoken man with a theoretical bent, who had served a lengthy sentence on Robben Island with Nelson Mandela, joined the NUM. Kgalema Motlanthe's recollection of his first encounter with Ramaphosa, as told to his biographer, Ebrahim Harvey, suggests that he viewed the NUM as a possible ally in the debate over how far left the ANC should lean: 'I did not know much about Cyril but we got on quite well. I could remember an article by Mono Badela on the Cosatu 1985 launch and the role Cyril played in the unity process leading up to it. I also tended to associate him with that banner at the 1987 NUM congress, "Freedom means socialism". The impact of seeing this slogan emblazoned at the congress had a powerful effect on us (on the Island). Those who were pushing for socialism in the debates now jumped up and said, "You see the workers are ready!"'[14]

Ramaphosa was equally enamoured of Motlanthe: 'I was struck by his analytical capabilities and powers and by his disciplined approach to everything. Here was someone who had great dignity and humility and was very keen to serve the union when he first joined.'[15] It was the beginning of a long-term entwinement between the NUM and the ANC. Ramaphosa would be succeeded by Motlanthe as general secretary. After Motlanthe, Gwede Mantashe would serve in the same position. All three – Ramaphosa, Motlanthe and Mantashe, in that order – would go on to serve as ANC secretary general.

There was the heady politics of alliance, but there was also the grind of building organisations from nothing. Jay Naidoo recalled another minor but revealing incident when, in 1987, he and Ramaphosa were inspecting a building, which had a view of Johannesburg's central business district, ahead of renting it: 'We proceeded to the landlord's office and were handed a thick legal document that we were asked to sign. "You are the lawyer, Cyril," I said. He had never signed a lease agreement before and neither had I. We perused the document, looked at each other, haggled about the rent and signed off.'[16] Cosatu House was to become the hub of trade union activity, and indeed a substantial part of the organisational backbone of the mass democratic movement in the final surge of protest against apartheid.

\*

In June 1986, Ramaphosa had his first face-to-face meeting with Harry Oppenheimer, South Africa's leading businessman and the man behind the mining companies where Ramaphosa was building the mineworkers' union. Oppenheimer was the face of South African business, and presided over Anglo American's vast mining and industrial empire, which dominated the Johannesburg Stock Exchange.

The occasion for their meeting was the first anniversary cele-
bration of the *Weekly Mail* (now the *Mail & Guardian*), a strongly
anti-apartheid newspaper that was independent of the major newspaper houses. Anton Harber, the *Weekly Mail*'s founding co-editor,
recalled: 'We wanted to do something rare and constructive: show
that two very different men in the middle of the toughest political
battles of the time could share a platform and show appreciation
for the role of the media. This was long before the ANC met a
business delegation; it was a time when the business-trade union
relationship was deeply hostile.'[17]

Harber writes that Ramaphosa arrived 'with a shaggy beard
looking every bit the fiery young revolutionary'.[18] Oppenheimer,
on the other hand, 'was a liberal of the distinctly South African
kind. He supported a free market and opposed apartheid, was a
great philanthropist and supporter of the white parliamentary
opposition, but operated a business that benefited fundamentally
from cheap migrant labour.'[19]

The two were supposed to talk about freedom of the media, but
Ramaphosa instead delivered a 'fierce and rousing denunciation
of the mining bosses, the conditions of mineworkers and the political situation, delivered in the Marxist language and with the rhe-
torical flourishes of the trade union movement'. As he spoke,
mineworkers and union officials who were present cheered loudly.
Harber writes that 'Oppenheimer looked uncomfortable. When he
got to his feet, he had to deal with aggressive chanting, singing
and dancing – until Ramaphosa signalled to his followers to let
Oppenheimer speak.' Oppenheimer said: 'We have just listened to
a long and impassioned speech from Mr Ramaphosa, made more
impassioned by the absence of fact.'[20] He followed this startling
assertion with some comments against the government's assault
on freedoms under the state of emergency.

Ramaphosa with Harry Oppenheimer in 1986.
The two would have a famous public confrontation at a function
organised by the *Weekly Mail*. (Robert Botha/*Business Day*)

The two men would soon become embroiled in one of the most bitter labour conflicts ever. Five years after it had been established, the NUM made the fateful decision to embark on a full national strike across the mining industry. The political context in which the strike took place was grim. The apartheid government had declared its second state of emergency in June 1986. It was aimed at quelling growing 'unrest', a euphemism for the mass grassroots uprising led by the UDF and Cosatu. Ramaphosa and other ANC-aligned union leaders had placed workers at the forefront of protests. With their putatively legal structures in place across the country, the trade unions were able to make up for the organisational weaknesses of the anti-apartheid civic, youth and community organisations in the broad front, which was the target of mass detentions and state-sanctioned killings.

The country's labour relations environment was fraught. In 1986 alone, some 1.3 million 'man days' were lost to strike action.[21] Mineworkers were in the thick of the strike action, with 35 000 workers striking at Gold Fields and other strikes at Gencor and elsewhere.

Within four years of winning bargaining recognition in 1983, the NUM had grown to 344 000 members. At its congress in February 1987, the union adopted the somewhat ominous slogan 'The Year Mineworkers Take Control'.[22] Television footage of the congress shows workers standing in orderly rows singing the somewhat maudlin struggle songs that marked formal occasions during the 1980s resistance. They are behind banners bearing the names of places across the country where mining of some sort takes place – Namaqualand, Phalaborwa, Witbank, Orange Free State, Carletonville.

In an advertisement in the *Weekly Mail*, the union declared: 'Let it be known once and for all that the source of conflict is rooted in the institutions of oppression and exploitation that exist in the mining industry. The hostel system, migrant labour and induna system were pioneered at the turn of the century by mineworkers' lives. It is from this brutal and draconian system that the AAC (Anglo American Corporation) has benefited. Over time these structures have been refined but kept intact. AAC has identified and acknowledges some of the issues which have caused the tensions. But what has it done? AAC wants industrial relations to be sound and orderly yet it is not prepared to remove the archaic structures which are the source of the conflict. It wants to publicly articulate its liberal views and distance itself from the violence and deaths, when the very cause of the problems emanates from the institutions it has created.'[23]

A few weeks after the congress, Ramaphosa presented the Chamber of Mines – the mining industry employers' body – with the union's demands: a 30 per cent wage increase, the abolition of migrant labour and improved hostel accommodation.[24] Fate would have it that Bobby Godsell, the negotiating partner with whom

Ramaphosa had done many deals, was away in Boston for the duration of the talks. In his place was Peter Gush, who had just taken charge of labour negotiations for the Chamber.

As was the custom, the Chamber simply ignored the first round of demands, probably believing them to be the usual inflated demands that precede more rational discussions. Two months later, when talks finally got under way, the Chamber got a shock. The NUM now demanded wage increases of between 40 and 55 per cent, as well as better danger pay, more holidays and death benefits. The Chamber responded with a wage offer of 12.5 per cent.

Negotiations ground on for a while, and the gap between the two sides narrowed substantially. But Gush would not budge. According to Godsell, 'Peter had decided that the gap at half a per cent was not something he wanted to think about. He thought they were revolutionaries. He was determined to put his stamp of authority down. He wanted to smash the union and the union wanted to smash management.'[25] There was a deadlock, and the NUM decided to take the next step and ballot its members over a strike.

On the eve of this momentous decision, Ramaphosa got together with Jay Naidoo at the house of unionist Howie Gabriels. Ramaphosa wanted to canvass the consequences of a sectorwide strike: 'We finished a bottle of whisky and opened another, talking into the early hours of the morning. The mining industry was the core of the apartheid state. It was like a state within a state: it had its own army, its own rules, its own police force, its own system of recruitment, its own authority and vast resources at its disposal. We knew the industry would move very heavily and considerable attention had to be paid to detail.'[26]

Suddenly the mining industry was in the throes of its greatest ever turmoil. On 2 August 1987, out of the 210 000 mineworkers who voted, some 95 per cent backed a strike. The NUM called for a national strike to begin on the evening of Sunday 9 August.[27] On Monday 10 August, the first official day of the strike, some 340 000 mineworkers downed tools. This represented no less than 70 per cent of black workers in the coal and gold industries. It was a phenomenal achievement for a union that had not existed five years earlier.

At a press briefing early on in the strike, a bearded Ramaphosa wore the red and black tracksuit top of the NUM. Seated to his left was his deputy, Marcel Golding, and to his right was the union's president, James Motlatsi. Addressing the media, Ramaphosa cut a serious figure: 'At present, we've got 340 000 miners on strike at 44 gold and coal mines – that is in the Free State and the Transvaal. The areas are Klerksdorp, Carletonville, Secunda, Witbank, Witwatersrand and the Free State. The dignity and discipline has been marred by a number of actions that have been taken by mine management against our members together with their trusted allies, the South African Police.' At a separate meeting in Evaton, Motlatsi said: 'The Chamber is the elephant and we are the mosquito. The mosquito will kill the elephant. At this time, your hearts should not feel pain. Don't be confused. If your hearts feel pain and you get confused, we will lose this war. The executive ordered that all the resources of our union, all the workers of our union and all the officials of our union must come together to win this war. I would rather be buried in my grave than lose this war.'

It was fighting talk, and there were times when the strike did seem like a war, as brutal violence began to be reported. The mining companies had large security detachments complete with armoured vehicles and riot control capacity. It was not long before the mining houses were being accused of violently attacking strikers to sow disunity. One mineworker recalled: '... those boers rammed the gate with the Hippos, broke it open, and rode into the hostel. They said over the loudspeakers, "Now we are taking control, no one is going to control again, you are too late with your controlling." They told us to go to our rooms, and then they just started to attack us with their dangerous weapons, shooting at us, without even giving us five minutes, using teargas, rubber bullets and pistols with proper bullets. When we were in our rooms, they turned off the water, and they stopped food from coming in. At nine o'clock that night, they told us to come out, we are going to work now. They shot teargas into the rooms, and chased us out with batons, and forced us to stand in line. They then forced us into the lifts at gunpoint, and we were faced with no choice but to go underground, all the shifts at once, and also the surface workers, forced down underground at gunpoint.'[28]

It was inevitable that the dispute would become politicised. As the strike entered its second week, Ramaphosa again addressed the media, saying: 'It is clear that the state has taken the decision to intervene in our strike with the view of undermining it and have taken the decision to come on the employers' side. It is clear they are going to make a concerted effort to try and crush the strike and try and crush it in a military way.'

Alongside this repression was the response of the mine owners in the form of the mass dismissal of workers. Television footage shows a young Bobby Godsell, back from his overseas sojourn, explaining the owners' point of view: 'Liberal business is trying to find a sustainable pattern of sharing power with black workers. A pattern of sharing power that does justice to economic reality and that is fair in terms of everybody's interests . . . My under-standing of a strike is that it's not there to destroy an employer or the enterprise. And we have already approached that level in this strike. Two of our shafts have been closed permanently. Those jobs are lost forever.' Ramaphosa countered with: 'There's no such thing as a liberal bourgeois – they are all the same. They use fascist methods to destroy workers' lives and in the end, we came up with the conclusion that there has never been a liberal image to Anglo's existence. It's all been just a façade and this has been exposed to our members.'[29]

On the other side of the fence, striking workers turned on those who did not support the strike, sometimes with deadly consequences. Kangaroo courts handed down the death sentence to some who refused to participate. Did Ramaphosa share some of the blame for these killings, by failing to rein in the union's more aggressive members, or was the strike now out of the NUM's control? Asked for his view, Michael Spicer told me: 'He's been consistent in the sense that he's absolutely ruthless. The ends justify the means and sometimes the ends can be ruthless.'

The politicisation of the strike was not helped by the action of the ANC's union arm, Sactu, which chose to announce in the midst of the strike that it was in control and that workers would not return to work until apartheid had been dismantled. The NUM was placed in the uncomfortable position of having to reassure the Chamber that there was no truth to the Sactu statement and that workers would return to work if their wage demands were met.[30]

Ramaphosa also had a sense of the dramatic. Godsell told me how, at a meeting to discuss the growing violence related to the strike, Ramaphosa deliberately arrived late: 'He threw down rubber bullets on the table and said: "Baas Godsell, is this your concept of minimum force?"'

After three weeks of strike action, nine workers were dead, 500 had been injured and 400 had been arrested. Anglo American took the next step to end the strike, dismissing between 50 000 and 60 000 workers and threatening to do the same to the rest of the workforce.

Things had become desperate. Ramaphosa, Godsell and other negotiators convened for a seven-hour session on 25 August, the 19th day of the strike. After the meeting, Ramaphosa, wearing a white shirt and grey blazer, made a sombre announcement: 'We met the Chamber today and the Chamber presented proposals to us on two issues. The Chamber refused to make an offer on wages, they refused to make an offer on June 16. They also refused to make an offer on danger pay as well as holiday leave where we had demanded 30 days per annum. Our negotiating team has decided that this offer should be taken back to our membership team on all the mines. Mine management have agreed that meetings should be held on all the mines where workers are on strike so that workers can have the opportunity of considering the offer on their own and decide whether to reject or accept.'[31]

After report-back meetings, talks resumed on the day that marked three weeks into the strike. Ramaphosa later told waiting journalists: 'Today we've reached agreement with the Chamber – an agreement that has brought an end to the strike. The strike by over 340 000 mineworkers ends this evening officially.' He searched for a way to put a gloss on the outcome, which appeared to favour the Chamber, because few concessions had been made: 'The fact that the strike has lasted such a long period demonstrated the resilience and determination of our members to fight for a living wage. We have proved beyond any doubt that the National Union of Mineworkers enjoys the support of mineworkers and that no amount of harassment and attempts to break the strike have broken the unity and discipline of miners. It must be remembered that it was the mining industry and specifically the Chamber of Mines which pioneered the most oppressive features of apartheid South Africa which manifests itself through the migrant labour system, hostel systems and the pass system.' His soundbite? 'They have not won and we have not lost. What has happened instead is that they have helped the union build a strong foundation for further and significant victories in the future.'[32] The workers began to return to the stopes on 30 August.

Was the strike a colossal act of folly? Writing in the *New York Times*, veteran journalist John Battersby said: 'Some said it was a remarkable achievement that a five-year-old union had been able to conduct a three-week strike in such an authoritarian society without destroying itself. Previous mine strikes had collapsed within 48 hours.'[33] On the other hand, the union had put the industry through the financial grindstone and hundreds of millions of rands in revenue had been lost. And the workers failed to achieve their demands, settling for management's offer on wages and working conditions. Ramaphosa said the closing of shafts and the dismissal of tens of thousands of workers made it impossible to continue with the strike. Desperately seeking consolation for the decision to settle, he said: 'Our membership does not regard this as a defeat but rather as part of the struggle to win all the demands that have been set.'[34] He added a bitter note. Anglo American had used 'fascist methods' to destroy workers lives: 'Throughout this strike it has been clear that there is no such thing as a liberal bourgeois.'[35]

In Godsell's view, the strike was a disaster for the NUM: 'Cyril and the NUM leadership collectively massively misread the situation. They didn't believe for a moment that the workers would be laid off.' Once Anglo had taken this step, the strike was all but over. 'He lost the strike. He seriously lost the strike. Management won the strike but for the wrong reasons and in the wrong way.' In truth, there were no winners or losers. Anglo lost more gold production through the firing of the 50 000 workers than it did during the strike. Rebuilding the underground teams when workers were rehired took a full six months, leading to further losses in production.

Whatever the outcome of the strike, Ramaphosa had established himself as a formidable political force on the national stage. He had caught the eye of powerful leaders within the ANC. One of them was watching events closely from prison. Over the next decade, Nelson Mandela would identify Ramaphosa as a future leader and a great political battle would unfold.

# THREE

# Mandela's chosen one

It was fairly simple and straightforward. Yes, it is true that
Madiba had wanted me to play that role, but he had to consult
other people and it was entirely within his right to consult a
number of people and those people felt that I was still too young.
– *Cyril Ramaphosa*

When the struggle to end apartheid reached its climax in the late
1980s, Ramaphosa was positioned to take a great political leap
forward. The front against apartheid consisted of three broad
camps. There were the 'exiles', who were operating abroad either
as diplomats mobilising public opinion and foreign governments
against apartheid or as members of the armed exile army, Umkhonto we Sizwe, which operated from states sympathetic to the
ANC such as Angola and Zambia. There were the 'islanders' –
named after the apartheid political prison, Robben Island, off Cape
Town – who included Nelson Mandela and others serving lengthy
sentences for treason and other major offences. And then there
were the 'internals', who mobilised communities behind the UDF
and Cosatu. Following the intense repression of the mid-1980s,
the UDF and Cosatu began to work interchangeably under the
banner of the mass democratic movement.

By the time Mandela was released in February 1990, Ramaphosa
had become a leading figure among the internals as the general
secretary of the NUM, Cosatu's largest union at the time. More than
that, he had played a leading role in the formation of Cosatu and,
more especially, in aligning it with the ANC.

Mandela's jail conditions were substantially relaxed in the months leading up to his release from Victor Verster prison, near Paarl. He was moved into one of the warders' cottages on the property, where he was permitted to meet with members of the mass democratic movement. Ramaphosa first encountered Mandela on one of these visits in late 1989, where he apparently made a good impression: 'I received ANC people from all the regions, as well as delegates from the UDF and Cosatu. One of these young men was Cyril Ramaphosa, the general secretary of the National Mine Workers' Union and one of the ablest of the new generation of leadership.'[1] Ramaphosa was among the members of the reception committee on hand when Mandela emerged from prison on 11 February 1990.

Mandela recalled the meeting at the cottage before his release: 'A number of comrades from the Reception Committee, including Cyril Ramaphosa and Trevor Manuel, were at the house bright and early. I wanted initially to address the people of Paarl, who had been very kind to me during my incarceration, but the reception committee was adamant that that would not be a good idea.'[2]

Jay Naidoo recalls the chaos that engulfed the newly released Mandela: 'Out of sight, you could hear the roar of more crowds, curious, joyful and impatient. We were extremely nervous about his safety as the state had abandoned the responsibility for Mandela's security and we had to act as his only bodyguards. Madiba and Winnie had been seated in a modest sedan, the best car we could organise, which belonged to someone Trevor Manuel knew and was driven by a Cape Town activist called Sonto. Cyril, Valli [Moosa] and I were piled into Trevor's beaten-up Toyota.'[3]

Mandela made his first public appearance on the balcony of the Cape Town City Hall. At his side stood Ramaphosa. It was a difficult political moment. Mandela explained that he had been talking to the apartheid government: 'My talks with the government have been aimed at normalising the political situation in the country. We have not as yet begun discussing the basic demands of the struggle.' He went on to say: 'I wish to stress that I myself have at no time entered into negotiations about the future of our country except to insist on a meeting between the ANC and the government.'[4]

Ramaphosa was at Mandela's side in his capacity as the chairman of the National Reception Committee, a body set up to coordinate the activities that followed Mandela's release. His proximity to Mandela at this crucial moment played no small part in elevating his profile, leading to speculation that he might be destined for greater things.

Ramaphosa's access to Mandela was no political accident. He was viewed by the left within the ANC, which was suspicious of Mbeki's accommodating centrism, as a potential future leader. Mbeki's base among the 'nationalist' exiles was unhappy with this, and a behind-the-scenes tussle ensued over who had access to Mandela and who, by extension, would one day have his blessing to take over the leadership.

Ramaphosa had the early running with Mandela, but by 1991 he had all but disappeared from his side. It was Mbeki who wrote all of Mandela's speeches in 1990 and 1991. Was Ramaphosa outmanoeuvred by a more calculating opponent? Mbeki's biographer, Mark Gevisser, has a more sanguine explanation: 'Some of Mbeki's detractors suggest that he "iced" or "dumped" Ramaphosa. More likely, he simply outpaced the trade unionist: no one else had Mbeki's stamina for – and experience in – the life out of hotel rooms that Mandela's grand global circuit required.'[5]

*

In July 1991, the pendulum appeared to swing the other way when Ramaphosa accomplished a major political coup, defeating the former exiles Alfred Nzo and Jacob Zuma to be elected ANC secretary general at the party's first conference inside the country, in Durban. Ramaphosa's decision to stand against Nzo and Zuma broke the unspoken exile pattern of such leaders being informally agreed on prior to the vote, an opaque process that had become habit because of the party's need to operate clandestinely while in exile.

Ramaphosa enjoyed the support of the SACP and its highly influential leader, Joe Slovo, whom he had encountered in that Lusaka hotel room all those years ago. Mandela apparently approved of his election, saying: 'Cyril Ramaphosa was elected secretary general, evidence that the torch was being passed from an older generation of leadership to a younger one. Cyril, whom I met only upon my release from prison, was a worthy successor to a long line of notable ANC leaders. He was probably the most accomplished negotiator in the ranks of the ANC.'[6] Leaving aside the fact that Mandela's memory of his first meeting with Ramaphosa while he was still in Victor Verster appeared to have become muddled with the latter's role at his release, it is clear that he was impressed with Ramaphosa's negotiating skills.

Despite the already existing strains, the Ramaphosa-Mbeki relationship was not entirely broken; Mark Gevisser relates this moment of comradely brotherhood between the two: 'The conference was scheduled to close on Sunday 8 July. But in the early hours of the morning of this final day, the debate on resolutions found itself deadlocked, once more, around the issue of sanctions. The environment of the conference – comrades stirred into heightened militancy by their collective mass – could not have been more hostile to Mbeki and his ideas . . . Ramaphosa, the newly elected secretary general, sidled up to Mbeki and said, "Chief, you'd better take over. You're going to lose this battle."'[7] Mbeki eventually took the floor and delivered a powerful statement that sealed the debate.

But Ramaphosa's deference to Mbeki's oratorical prowess was just one moment in a relationship that grew ever more bitter. Not long after the conference, Ramaphosa moved decisively against Mbeki and Zuma. As Gevisser tells it, what can only be described as a 'palace coup' took place in August while Mandela was away on a trip to Cuba and Mbeki and Zuma were at a conference in Cambridge: 'Zuma heard about it on the BBC and went rushing over to tell his comrade: the new man, Ramaphosa, had convened the NWC [National Working Committee] while they were away, and had sidelined them!'[8] Zuma lost his position as ANC intelligence chief and was replaced by UDF leader Mosiuoa Lekota, while Mbeki was replaced as head of negotiations by Ramaphosa himself.

It was perhaps at this point that some of the exiles became wary of Ramaphosa, who had become a palpable threat to their hegemony within the ANC. It was, for the first time, conceivable that the leaders of the internal democratic forces might take over the ANC. Ramaphosa was no longer simply the man who held Mandela's umbrella. He was now a potential heir apparent. The political rivalry between Mbeki and Ramaphosa had been ignited and would burn fiercely for two decades.

At the Durban conference, Mandela had been elected ANC president, with fellow Robben Island inmate Walter Sisulu as his deputy. Oliver Tambo, by now ailing, was elected national chairperson. Jacob Zuma would deputise for Ramaphosa as deputy secretary general. One name notably absent from the top leadership structure was that of Thabo Mbeki.

Shortly after taking up his new duties, in August 1991, Ramaphosa was interviewed by the Irish researcher Padraig O'Malley. O'Malley spent several years travelling to South Africa to conduct some 2 000 hours of interviews with political figures on both sides. These interviews now stand as an invaluable record of the thinking of key players during the transition from apartheid to democracy.

Ramaphosa replied to a question about how he was using his time: 'We are in the ANC going through a period of reorganising, restructuring the organisation and in the process of doing that we are setting up systems and so forth and you find that you get embroiled in a whole lot of things, you get involved in many things that keep you engaged on a daily basis, on an hourly basis and I have found that you do so many things at the same time that you hardly ever have time to take a moment's breath. You don't even get enough time to sit down, to reflect on the many things that you are doing and happening around you. I am just hoping that this is a transitory type of phenomenon and once the restructuring has been completed the workload that rests on my shoulders now will reduce somewhat and I will then be able to take enough time on a daily basis to think, to plan, to strategise and to have a whole range of people doing what I am doing now. I think that is the most effective way of operating as what in the business world they would call an executive officer of a company.'[9]

The idea that the ANC secretary general could compare himself to 'an executive officer in a company' was a signal that Ramaphosa was planning to do things very differently within the party. It was clear that he intended to break the hold of the 'need-to-know' politics of the exiled movement on the leadership, and to replace it with a more modern, transparent and efficient structure. To those who were hoping to benefit, perhaps illicitly, when the ANC took over government, this must have been an unappetising prospect. From now on, much more attention would be paid to the man whom Mandela favoured as his successor.

*

Ramaphosa, it seemed, had won the day. But it was not to be. As suddenly and surprisingly as he had risen to a position of strength, he lost ground to Mbeki as the date drew near for the formation of a new government after the first democratic election. Ramaphosa had been elected as ANC secretary general, but power was already slipping out of his hands within the party.

Mandela had to choose who would serve as his deputy president in government. He chose Mbeki. The episode is recounted by William Mervyn Gumede: 'Mandela had personally canvassed ANC provincial branches to re-elect Ramaphosa, but in the run-up to the conference, Mbeki supporters had launched an all-out attempt to shove Ramaphosa to the margins and ensure that the way was open for their man to consolidate his power unchallenged. Despite the 1991 ANC conference triumph, the presidency still slipped out of Ramaphosa's hands. Even Mandela's partisan support counted for nothing.'[10] Gumede has a simple explanation for how Mbeki won out: 'How had the decision been made? Just as Jawaharlal Nehru had been singled out for leadership when the Congress Party of India took power after independence in 1947, Mbeki was anointed by the ANC's elders.'[11]

The man who would become Mandela's director general in the Presidency, Jakes Gerwel, confirmed that Mandela had favoured Ramaphosa, but maintained that Ramaphosa's competence as an administrator was not the only factor considered: 'Mischievous deductions are sometimes made from his disclosure that he proposed Cyril Ramaphosa rather than Thabo Mbeki as deputy president to the ANC's senior officials in 1994. This proposal in fact had little to do with the respective merits of the two men – both of whom he holds in high regard as hugely capable leaders – but with his concern about allegations of Xhosa dominance while a non-Xhosa of Ramaphosa's capabilities was available.'[12]

Ramaphosa was by now very much in the Mandela mould, working hard to reconcile black and white South Africans. The political commentator Richard Calland recalls his first encounter with Ramaphosa at Cape Town's Baxter Theatre: 'The audience was middle-aged as well as middle-class and almost entirely white. There was a buzz of nervous anticipation, which fell into a deathly hush as Ramaphosa walked in. Standing, he looked them in the eyes, paused, released his gentle smile and said – I will never forget the words – "In a few weeks, we are all going to make history together." He paused and the audience let out a sigh of relief. People looked around; did he say "we"? We are going to make history together? Really? Not "them" making it for "us".'[13]

When I spoke to Ramaphosa some twenty years later, in 2013, he said he believed Mandela wanted him to be his deputy president but had been countermanded after consulting senior figures in the party: 'It was fairly simple and straightforward. Yes, it is true that Madiba had wanted me to play that role, but he had to consult other people and it was entirely within his right to consult a number of people and those people felt that I was still too young.'

When we spoke, a long time had passed since this political fracture and Ramaphosa offered a reconciliatory view of this decision: 'With hindsight, I agree with them, I was young. If I had taken that role, at 60 I would have been out. I would have been out, I would have served two terms and that would have been the end – at 60. And I still have unbelievable strength to carry on.'

According to this version, the position taken was that Ramaphosa should wait his turn: 'That's what they argued. They argued, and I would say correctly, that there were more senior comrades in the ANC like Thabo Mbeki, Jacob Zuma and so forth, and then I think my, if you like, junior status, militated against me and Madiba chose a much more senior and experienced person by any definition, Thabo.' Ramaphosa said he saw the reasoning for the decision: Mbeki was 'ten years older than me, had much longer tenure in the ANC, and had also been in the top leadership positions of the ANC having worked with Oliver Tambo for a long time'.

Ramaphosa recalled the conversation with Mandela, which went along these lines:

> Mandela: Look, this is what I have decided. I would like you to get into the Cabinet as Minister of Foreign Affairs.
> Ramaphosa: I actually would prefer to remain in the party to do what I have been elected to do which is to build the party.

Mandela listened as Ramaphosa explained that this task had been interrupted by the negotiation process when he had been asked to lead the negotiating team.

> Ramaphosa: Please allow me to remain in the party.
> Mandela: Fine.

An agreement was struck that Ramaphosa would stay out of Cabinet and continue as ANC secretary general instead. But was it quite as simple as Ramaphosa recalled in hindsight? Kader Asmal agreed that Ramaphosa had been Mandela's chosen successor and ought to have been deputy president or, at least, a senior minister: 'For many of us, including me, Ramaphosa was a shoo-in for Deputy President and was clearly Mandela's chosen heir. Instead of the capable Ramaphosa, we got Alfred Nzo as Foreign Minister.'[14]

One big clue that Ramaphosa was not entirely happy with the way things panned out following the 1994 election was his decision to skip Mandela's inauguration. For the secretary general of the ANC to miss the swearing-in of Nelson Mandela, perhaps the greatest political event in the country's history, was astonishing. It suggested that Ramaphosa was more than piqued at being overlooked and wished to show his displeasure. If this was so, it was an act of petulance that suggests a weakness in Ramaphosa's character. While his single-minded determination and his ability to impose his character on others during the negotiations had been a strength, it now seemed to be double-edged sword.

\*

No sooner had the dust settled after the inauguration and the appointment of the new Cabinet than Mandela once again called on Ramaphosa, this time to play a leading role in finalising the Interim Constitution. The document had to form the basis of a further set of negotiations to produce a final constitution, which all had agreed needed to be passed by a democratically elected parliament.

Mandela, much caricatured as a genial reconciler, may have harboured a deep political insight. He had been made to trust Mbeki as his deputy, but he wanted the final Constitution to be driven to its conclusion by someone who shared his vision of a rights-driven document. Whatever his motivation, Mandela was insistent and Ramaphosa simply could not refuse. He recalls that Mandela told him: '"You can't say no, you've got to take this position and be chairman of the constitution-making body. There is no one else that I could have as chairman of this important body." So, I accepted that, which really interrupted once again the task that I had wanted to execute with relish, of building ANC structures. And it was largely because of the experience that I had had in the NUM.'

Jay Naidoo believes that Ramaphosa lost the leadership battle within the ANC because he was distracted by the constitutional negotiations: 'Cyril's commitment to the negotiations was also to be the undoing of his goal to succeed Mandela. Cyril neglected the corridor politics of the ANC while others were busy building a base from which to seize political power within the ANC. Cyril was not alone in not understanding that lesson.'[15]

Ramaphosa, now ANC secretary general, with Cosatu's Jay Naidoo
at a media briefing in July 1992. (Gallo Images/Media24 Archive/Denis Farrell)

Ramaphosa fought and lost on the national political stage. But he became the man most responsible for South Africa's crowning achievement, a democratic, human-rights based Constitution that remains the single most important defender of the people. How he pulled this off remains one of democratic South Africa's most compelling stories.

# FOUR

# *The big deal*

His relaxed manner and convivial expression were contradicted by
coldly calculating eyes, which seemed to be searching
continuously for the softest spot in the defences of his opponents.
His silver tongue and honeyed phrases lulled potential victims
while his arguments relentlessly tightened around them.
– *FW de Klerk*

While the leadership tussles within the ANC raged on, Ramaphosa
had more pressing matters to attend to. Mandela's release from
prison in February 1990 had led to the start of negotiations between the ANC and the governing National Party of President FW
de Klerk. As negotiations between bitter adversaries go, the talks
would probably have been rated 'least likely to succeed' when they
began. In the end, they succeeded spectacularly, ending racial discrimination and introducing democracy under one of the world's
most progressive constitutions into a country with the world's most
serious racial divide.

There were many factors that contributed to the success of the
series of talks that began in 1990 and culminated in the adoption
of the final constitution in 1996. By 1990, the apartheid government had exhausted its capacity to repress the popular uprising
against it using the security forces, and increasing numbers of
young white South Africans refused to serve in the South African
Defence Force (I can say with pride that I was one of them). The
internal uprising, led by the ANC-aligned UDF, had begun to take
command of the streets with large protest gatherings. The state's

financial room for manoeuvre was severely restricted by the refusal of global lenders to roll over loans, and foreign investment had dried up as international sanctions bit hard. The ANC had reached the limits of what it could achieve through the strategy of armed struggle. It was unable to convert the 'armed propaganda' of exploding bombs into a properly supported internal guerrilla network of the strength and scale necessary to challenge the state. Much of the militant activity within the country, such as the assaults on illegitimate 'puppet' municipal councils, was, in any event, the product of street committees and the like that had no direct relationship with the ANC's armed wing, Umkhonto we Sizwe. Both parties recognised that they had entered into a protracted stalemate, the outcome of which was uncertain but which would certainly cost many lives and severely damage the country's economy and infrastructure.

At its July conference, the ANC had resolved that Ramaphosa would head up a Negotiations Commission along with four other senior leaders. In August 1991, fresh from his upset victory in the election battle for ANC secretary general, Ramaphosa explained to Padraig O'Malley his perspective on the coming constitutional talks: 'Five National Working Committee people have been put in charge of that and I have been charged with the responsibility of heading that Negotiations Commission. In that commission, you've got people who already are working out an idea of the course of negotiations with the government and the various phases that negotiations must go through. No doubt the first phase is to be prepared ourselves in our own ranks and we are now in the phase of consultation, thorough consultation with our constituencies on the strategic shift that was effected a few weeks ago by our National Executive with regard to our approach to negotiations.'[1]

The strategic shift referred to was the move from less formal agreements on the terms and conditions of talks to the actual grind of negotiations. Before, the ANC had been all about removing obstacles to talks – securing the release of prisoners and the return of exiles, ending violence and reducing security legislation. Now it would be all about shifting power from the old government to a new transitional authority and an interim constitution so that democratic elections could take place freely and fairly. 'It became clear to us that that was the obstacle, the main obstacle is the government and you've got to remove the government because once you remove the government then all the other obstacles are removed. It's like a jigsaw puzzle, so you solve one and everything else falls into place,' Ramaphosa told O'Malley.[2]

For those across the table at the talks, Ramaphosa represented a more difficult challenge. His years of experience of gruelling wage negotiations with South Africa's mining bosses had honed his bargaining skills. Ramaphosa understood that compromise was essential. But he understood another vital plank of negotiations: you had to build yourself into a position of strength if the compromise was to favour you. Each compromise had to be made only when the terrain had shifted in your favour. Ramaphosa was, in reality, the only ANC leader with experience at the coalface of tough negotiation.

*

For the four years between 1990 and 1994, Ramaphosa would once more be the man across the table at negotiations; this time, the apartheid government and its allies would be seated on the other side. The stakes would be very high indeed. On the table was the shape of post-apartheid South Africa for decades to come.

If the ANC had little experience in negotiating, so too did the National Party, which had become, under PW Botha, an authoritarian militarist state. In the words of Bobby Godsell: 'The Afrikaner nationalists were much more useless negotiators. It was not a dream deferred but a dream exhausted. They had no plan B.'

The National Party knew it had a tougher opponent in Rama-phosa than they would have had in Thabo Mbeki. Apartheid intelligence boss Niël Barnard puts it this way: 'Why was Cyril Ramaphosa the one chosen to lead the ANC team, and not Thabo Mbeki, who, after all, had done the lion's share of the prepara-tion?'[3] The answer, he says, lay in the dynamics within the ANC: 'The NI [National Intelligence] sources gave a logical explanation for this, which lay partly in the internal conflict in the ANC – con-flict between the decimated United Democratic Front (UDF) wing inside the country and the corrupt external wing. The former had been manhandled by security forces; the latter's members were gallivanting overseas in posh hotels. This was the perception, and was not entirely devoid of the truth.'[4]

Barnard continues: 'The ANC leadership regarded Mbeki as the talented intellectual who might be too soft in his dealings with the government, too malleable. In contrast, Ramaphosa was seen as the battering ram who would put the government's negotiators in their place. When the pendulum swung in favour of aggressive negotiators, Ramaphosa, with his personality and his experience in trade union bargaining, seemed the obvious choice.'[5]

The strength of FW de Klerk's negotiating position stemmed from the sweeping concessions he had made at the outset – un-banning the ANC, SACP and PAC, releasing Mandela and other Robben Islanders and reaching out to talk to the ANC. These steps – or at least the pace with which they had been made – took the ANC by surprise. It had to scramble to play catch-up, dis-cussing the merits of talks and attempting to reconcile its mili-tants with those who were ready to talk.

De Klerk had managed to put some distance between himself and his party's right – the so-called securocrats, who had engi-neered successive states of emergency and military repression through the 1980s. It was widely reported that the likes of Defence

Ramaphosa, Thabo Mbeki (second row), Nelson Mandela and
Jacob Zuma at the Codesa talks in Johannesburg.
(Graeme Williams/South Photographs/Africa Media Online)

minister Magnus Malan were unhappy with his progressive stance.
As if to drive home his determination to take a radical new direction, on 30 July 1991 he replaced Malan with Roelf Meyer. Malan,
the former Chief of the South African Defence Force, was igno-
miniously moved to the portfolio of Water Affairs and Forestry,
about as far as you could get from the military.

De Klerk was already a long way down the reform track. He
would have to be slowed down, hauled in and overtaken. The first
step in this process would be to force him to own his party, including those with whom he was at war. The opportunity had first
presented itself when the Inkathagate scandal broke. A disillu-
sioned policeman leaked police documents to the *Weekly Mail*
showing that the security police were funding Inkatha via a secret
account known only to its leader, Mangosuthu Buthelezi.

In the August 1991 interview with Padraig O'Malley, Ramaphosa outlined how the Inkathagate scandal would be used to paint a less favourable picture of the De Klerk government: 'Inkathagate has actually given much more proof, I think, to many other people that this government is so corrupt, so much more illegitimate that it can never hope to continue, it shouldn't be allowed to continue governing even through the period of transition.' He elaborated: 'We're saying we must have a sovereign government that will be charged with the responsibility of ushering us peacefully, neutrally through the period of transition because transition, this big wide road that we see in front of us called transition, has a lot of potholes and we want to be steered properly on this road and avoid all the potholes.'[6]

*

One of the keys to the success of the talks was the relationship that developed between Ramaphosa and his National Party counterpart, Roelf Meyer. Meyer was one of the party's promising young leaders from its *verligte*, or enlightened, wing. He had encountered Ramaphosa before. As a deputy Law and Order minister, he had been the point man for the state during the 1987 mineworkers' strike. It is fair to say that the relationship had not exactly blossomed, as Ramaphosa had been adamant that the state had initiated violence against striking miners or else ignored it when it was perpetrated by the mine owners.

The circumstances had changed by the time they encountered one another again. In 1992, after just nine months as Defence minister, Meyer was transferred to the portfolio of Constitutional Development, which involved him more closely in the talks between the government and the ANC. Meanwhile, Ramaphosa had systematically demolished the man who sat opposite him at the negotiations on the proposed Bill of Rights. Tertius Delport, the

Deputy Minister of Constitutional Development, had been thrust into the limelight when the NP's previous chief negotiator, Gerrit Viljoen, had taken ill and retired from public life. I saw Delport's demolition first-hand, as I was the minutes secretary of this working group at Codesa. Ramaphosa had a habit of never addressing Delport directly. Instead, after driving him into a state of agitation by refusing to agree to anything he proposed, he would say: 'Mr Chairman, Dr Delport is becoming very emotional. I would appeal to you, Mr Chairman, to ask Dr Delport to control his emotions.' It was too much for Delport and, when the negotiations advanced to the next phase, Meyer replaced him as the NP's leading man.

Meyer readily concedes that he was at a disadvantage to Ramaphosa in the talks: 'He came with a lot of experience at that stage already, and built up his NUM experience when he was Secretary General of the National Union of Mineworkers for quite a long period of time during the 1980s,' he said in an interview many years later. 'So he had an advantage at the time that we started the constitutional discussions and negotiations.'[7]

Ramaphosa knew instinctively that Meyer was a negotiating partner he could trust. To Meyer, he was a 'reasonable person, very reasonable in terms of understanding where the other side is coming from'.[8] An encounter between the two while trout fishing helped forge the trust. The incident was recorded by the late Allister Sparks: 'A friend invites the ANC's chief negotiator Cyril Ramaphosa and his opposite number Roelf Meyer fishing. When Meyer embeds a trout hook in his hand, Ramaphosa is the only one who can extract it.'[9] That moment, when Ramaphosa fed Meyer a stiff whisky before removing the hook, was but one of many that built the relationship into a political game-changer.

According to Meyer, '[t]hat fishing incident was just one of many, but it was indicative of the kind of relationship that we succeeded in building, the friendship that we have succeeded finally to build, and the chemistry that exists between us'.[10] But if Meyer saw a genuine friendship developing, Ramaphosa saw opportunity. His comments on trout fishing could just as well be a description of how he evaluated negotiation opponents: 'You need to know what they are feeding on and how they are behaving, then decide on a strategy.'[11]

Years later, he would tell Lesley Cowling, then writing for the *Mail & Guardian*, that 'the only contribution trout fishing made to the negotiations was that he learnt how his opposite number looked when he was anxious and in pain'. The trout fishing raised eyebrows within the ANC, where it was viewed as a bourgeois indulgence, but Ramaphosa had Mandela's permission to take up the sport. 'Trout fishing teaches you patience and to accept failure, because you can go out there and not catch anything. It's an important attribute in life – you may not always get what you want and trout fishing teaches you that', he told Cowling.[12]

When it came to the negotiations with Meyer, however, Ramaphosa got most of what he and the ANC wanted: a unitary state with a government of national unity for a limited term and a constitution that would relegate the NP to oblivion and allow parties of the non-racial centre, such as the ANC, to dominate.

Once Ramaphosa had established that Meyer was not going to support a dilution of democracy with the NP's old 'group rights' message, he was prepared to deal with him. The moment when this occurred appears to have been when Meyer presented Ramaphosa with a draft paper by Francois Venter, an academic influential in Broederbond, and therefore NP, circles. Venter's paper departed from the long-held NP view that group rights should somehow enjoy institutional protection: 'Where such a process was legally institutionalised, however, as in South Africa, the natural process of group formation took on the characteristics of external and unacceptable force.'[13] According to Meyer, 'Cyril's eyes lit up' when he read the paper. After that, 'it was plain sailing'.[14]

Ramaphosa's relationship with Meyer served a practical purpose too. When the Codesa talks broke down after the Boipatong massacre in June 1992, it seemed that the constitutional negotiations might grind to a halt altogether. Four days after the massacre, Nelson Mandela addressed a large crowd in Evaton, saying that 'the negotiation process is completely in tatters'.[15] He told them: 'I instructed Ramaphosa that he and his delegation will not have any further discussions with the regime.'[16] Ramaphosa himself issued a harshly worded statement on the government's violent duplicity: 'It pursues a strategy which embraces negotiations, together with systematic covert actions, including murder, involving its security forces and surrogates.' He presented a long list of demands, including the creation of a representative constituent assembly to finalise the constitution. Until the government complied, 'the ANC has no option but to break off bilateral and Codesa negotiations'.[17]

Early in September, Ramaphosa was present when troops of the Ciskei homeland opened fire on demonstrators, killing 29. The decision to mount the protest was another of Ramaphosa's ploys to demonstrate the ANC's ability to mobilise in order to give him an advantage in the talks, when they resumed. After the shooting, the country was at a crisis point.

The public statements made by Ramaphosa and Mandela about all talks being off were a political white lie. While formal talks in the public spotlight had been called off, behind the scenes Ramaphosa and Meyer remained in close contact. Ramaphosa was at Mandela's side when the latter announced the suspension of talks. Minutes later, Meyer's phone rang. It was Ramaphosa, keeping the channel between the two parties open.

Meyer recalled the moment after the talks broke down: 'We knew we had a responsibility and we were both committed to that same goal. Of course, it was not always easy. I can recall the first talks after the Boipatong massacre. There was a complete breakdown of negotiations. We had to start from scratch, because there was nothing. And the next day we had to sit down, look at each other across the table and ask: "Where do we start from now?" And of course, there were demands that Cyril had on behalf of ANC and there were positions that I had to protect on behalf of the NP government.'[18]

Once the two had recognised that there was no alternative to finding a solution, they had no choice but to build trust. Meyer continued: 'It was extremely challenging times. Some evenings we walked out on each other. At the same time that was happening, we knew that the next day we had to sit down again – there was no other way. And I think that forced us into a relationship and an understanding of what he had to argue for and what I had to argue for. And that helped us – that understanding. In the end, it transformed into trust. I keep on thinking there are certain basic steps to develop trust. The first one is: you need to know one another, the second: you have to respect one another and the third: understand one another. That can then lead to basic trust. We had to go through those exercises and fortunately we were both open-minded enough to know that is what we needed to do and that is how it is going to work.'[19]

This ability to recognise and then elevate the larger shared goal above immediate differences was critical to the make-up of both Ramaphosa and Meyer. It played no small part in ensuring that the 'miracle' of the negotiated transition from apartheid to democracy succeeded. In another interview on the transition, Meyer put it like this: 'When we started, we didn't know each other. But it was more than that. We were actually enemies. We were not necessarily shooting each other or killing each other, but when we started to sit down as opponents at the table, we were enemies.' He went on: 'Strangely, there was not an enemy-like atmosphere, despite the fact that we were enemies.'[20] The relationship grew into a powerful tool that ensured that a negotiated solution would remain on track no matter what: 'That relationship between him and I was so powerful that at one stage we developed a line between us that said, "There's not a problem we can't resolve".'[21]

The close relationship between Ramaphosa and the National Party's Roelf Meyer was key to the success of the Codesa negotiations in 1993.
(David Goldblatt/South Photographs/Africa Media Online)

The extent of this relationship is described by Padraig O'Malley in his biography of Mac Maharaj: 'With the permission of their principals, Cyril Ramaphosa and Roelf Meyer, the head of government's negotiating team, established contact and put together small teams to work on a series of steps that would enable both sides to resume formal talks. Between June and September, when negotiations were supposedly suspended, Meyer and Ramaphosa, the "channel" met on forty-three occasions.'[22] That would mean an average of ten meetings a month – one every three days.

The Ramaphosa-Meyer relationship was crucial to solving otherwise intractable problems. The *Financial Times* journalist Patti Waldmeir observed: 'Both men are charming, but where Meyer is boyish and direct, Ramaphosa is more calculating. For him, charm is a tool of the trade; it is integral to the way he exerts personal power. Ramaphosa exposes and exploits people's weaknesses in the way that Mandela exploits their strengths. The two men were a formidable combination.'[23]

But it was not all smooth sailing. Mac Maharaj told Waldmeir how Ramaphosa had one day decided to put Meyer in his place: 'Ramaphosa recalls accusing Meyer of behaving like a "white man" . . . Meyer does not remember racism being mentioned. But they all remember that Ramaphosa savaged Meyer – that he went too far, that he knew he had done so, that he possibly regretted it, but that he emerged as the dominant partner.'[24]

This view of the manipulative Ramaphosa was held by former president FW de Klerk, who used these words: 'His relaxed manner and convivial expression were contradicted by coldly calculating eyes, which seemed to be searching continuously for the softest spot in the defences of his opponents. His silver tongue and honeyed phrases lulled potential victims while his arguments relentlessly tightened around them.'[25]

*

The breakdown in talks was resolved with the Record of Understanding crafted by Ramaphosa and Meyer and announced on 26 September 1992. This was achieved by putting aside the lengthy list of demands (14 points) and, instead, agreeing on a basic quid pro quo. The ANC got an undertaking that there would be a two-phase process that would see a democratically elected body approve the final constitution. The NP got an undertaking that there would first be a draft constitution incorporating certain 'constitutional principles' that would have to be included in the final constitution.[26] Once this breakthrough had occurred, the foundation had been laid for the finalisation of the Interim Constitution and the principles that would be carried into the final constitution.

At this point, Ramaphosa was the country's mover and shaker. He was very much the engineer of the new order, understanding when pressure should be applied and when it should be released, by turns cajoling, threatening and charming. If he appeared to be going out on a limb, he always did so with the support of key party leaders, such as Joe Slovo, who worked side by side with him during the talks. Slovo was the author of the 'sunset clause', a guarantee that old-order civil servants would not lose their jobs

The influential SACP general secretary Joe Slovo (centre) provided crucial backing to Ramaphosa during the Codesa negotiations. Slovo is shown here with his deputy, Chris Hani (right), and Cosatu president John Gomomo (left) in 1991.
(Gallo Images/Media24 Archives/*Die Burger*)

after the transition to a democratic order. The introduction of the sunset clause was a breakthrough that helped to seal the deal.

Describing Slovo at his memorial service in 1995, Ramaphosa revealed his view on compromise and principle, that it was possible to be pragmatic without giving up your core principles: 'Throughout the negotiations, JS never compromised himself, his principles or the positions of the movement. He may be the father of the sunset clause which gave birth to the government of national unity, but let it be known that he never compromised an iota of his convictions.'[27]

In the end, the ANC achieved the unthinkable – an undiluted one person, one vote democracy under a constitution that compelled the post-apartheid state to address the social injustices of the past and which had in place guarantees that the country could not slide backwards into authoritarianism. There were to be many late nights, many moments of public disagreement and many barbed words between the parties on opposite sides of the table, but, in the end, the relationship that had sprung from the Ramaphosa-Meyer collaboration ensured that the process would not falter.

Some months after they rescued the negotiations from the Boipatong breakdown, Ramaphosa and Meyer had to take refuge when Afrikaner right-wingers attacked the venue for the talks, the World Trade Centre in Kempton Park. Together with Joe Slovo, they were ushered into a small room to keep them safe while a mob led by Eugène Terre'Blanche, the leader of the AWB, or Afrikaner Resistance Movement, used an armoured vehicle to smash through the building's glass doors. If it was the intention of the right-wingers to stop the talks, then their action had the opposite effect. The negotiators got a very real feel for their common enemy on the extreme right.

A similar relationship was established at a technical level between the ANC's Mac Maharaj and the government's Fanie van der Merwe. They were responsible for drafting the final quid pro quo that led to agreement on the Interim Constitution. The ANC agreed that there would be an amnesty. In return, the NP and government agreed that there would be no veto in the Cabinet. It was to be the Cabinet of a government of national unity. Up to that point, NP and government negotiators had argued that smaller parties should have a veto over decisions taken in the Cabinet in order to make the unity pact effective. Maharaj recalled: 'We went back to the working group with the draft. Cyril then said, "Now before we finalise this thing and say we're done, let's go back to the cabinet question. Do you still have a problem because I want to tell you that we will not agree to any form of veto and troika control?" They looked at what Fanie and I had drafted, namely the section that said the cabinet would function in the spirit of seeking consensus, and when all else failed, take decisions in the normal way, that is, by majority decision. And they said, "We're satisfied." In the end we did not spend even five minutes on settling the issue of cabinet decision making at the follow-up meeting.'[28]

The following day, the resolution on these final issues was put before the negotiating chamber and adopted. It was 17 November, Ramaphosa's 40th birthday. The Interim Constitution was finalised ahead of the country's first democratic election, set for 27 April 1994.

*

The passage of the Constitution of the Republic of South Africa Act 200 of 1993, otherwise known as the Interim Constitution, was a remarkable event. An all-white Parliament consented to its own demise in a political act that has rarely been seen anywhere else in the world. The preamble to the Interim Constitution contained the deal struck between Ramaphosa and Meyer in the Record of Understanding. It spoke of the 'need to create a new order in which all South Africans will be entitled to a common South African citizenship in a sovereign and democratic constitutional state in which there is equality between men and women and people of all races so that all citizens shall be able to enjoy and exercise their fundamental rights and freedoms'. And, it said that 'in order to secure the achievement of this goal, elected representatives of all the people of South Africa should be mandated to adopt a new Constitution in accordance with a solemn pact recorded as Constitutional Principles'.[29]

The 33 principles were the guarantee that the final constitution would not depart from the unqualified universal franchise and that a human rights-based state, guided by a Bill of Rights, would continue in perpetuity. It included provisions that explained in detail how the relationship between the central, provincial and local governments would be shaped and how power would be exercised.

And, significantly, it compelled the drafters of the final constitution to include a Bill of Rights that was shaped by the Bill of Rights in Chapter 3 of the Interim Constitution. This included the sweeping clause: 'No person shall be unfairly discriminated against, directly or indirectly, and, without derogating from the generality of this provision, on one or more of the following grounds in particular: race, gender, sex, ethnic or social origin, colour, sexual orientation, age, disability, religion, conscience, belief, culture or language.'[30] The right to life, to dignity and to freedom and security are taken for granted now, but at that time they represented a massive victory for those who had been on the receiving end of institutionalised racism under apartheid. Freedom of speech and expression were protected, and those who had been dispossessed of their land would be entitled to claim restitution.

The Act also contained the provision that 'every person shall have the right to acquire and hold rights in property and, to the extent that the nature of the rights permits, to dispose of such rights'.[31] This clause would, in future, be criticised as a means of protecting white domination of land and the economy by securing property rights obtained under apartheid. Twenty or so years on, a furious debate would erupt over whether or not the Constitution was standing in the way of 'radical economic transformation'.

While Ramaphosa and Meyer were sealing the constitutional deal, a new political drama was unfolding that would draw Thabo Mbeki back into the talks. The Afrikaner right wing and Mangosuthu Buthelezi's Zulu nationalist movement, Inkatha, remained outside of the formal talks and were becoming a security concern. If they were not brought into the fold, they might derail the first democratic election.

Ramaphosa was dismissive of those outside the negotiations, believing they would lose influence if they stayed out of the process of launching a new democratic country. Mbeki took a different view: every effort had to be made to reach an inclusive agreement. Mbeki concluded a deal with Buthelezi that would allow Inkatha to rejoin the process, but he accomplished this by leaving out the question of the election date. Mark Gevisser recounted the incident in his biography of Mbeki: 'Mbeki thought he had finessed things by finding a way to move things forward while allowing Buthelezi to save face. But the deal was not acceptable to Ramaphosa, who exploded when he found out about it, and successfully petitioned Mandela to reject it.'[32] Ramaphosa said of this moment: 'Millions of people were geared up for their liberation, and if there had been any attempt to postpone the election I think the country would have blown up.'[33]

*

Once the Interim Constitution had been adopted, Ramaphosa's attention – and that of the ANC – turned to the election of April

1994. When the result was finally certified, the ANC had won a substantial majority of 62.6 per cent of the vote, with voter turnout at a staggering 19.5 million. (Twenty years later, only 18.6 million would cast their votes in the national election.[34]) Against most expectations – especially those of the establishment think-tanks – the National Party achieved just over 20 per cent and came nowhere near to threatening the ANC.

The Interim Constitution brought into life a Government of National Unity. Cabinet positions would have to be shared in proportion to the votes achieved, and De Klerk would become one of the country's new deputy presidents (along with Thabo Mbeki) by virtue of the fact that his party had achieved the second highest number of votes.

In December 1994, the ANC held its 49th national conference and Ramaphosa was returned as secretary general. His report to the conference focused on the completion of the negotiation process and the first democratic election. He boasted: 'The National Party government was effectively defeated at the negotiations table. They failed to realise their objectives through negotiations, and were forced by the combined strategies of the democratic movement to accede in a substantial way to the demands of the ANC.'[35] It was hard to argue against this view, as South Africa was now a free democratic country where each vote was equal.

Ramaphosa was to play no role in the new government, after turning down the offer of Foreign Affairs minister. He had been refused the deputy presidency and was now determined to stay out of government altogether. He claims that he had decided to return to ANC headquarters to continue with his duties as secretary general by strengthening the organisation, and that may well have been the case. But, as discussed in the previous chapter, he was prevailed upon by Mandela to chair the assembly that was to draft the final constitution.

The Constitutional Assembly consisted of all 490 legislators from both the houses of Parliament – the National Assembly and the Senate elected in the first democratic election. They were tasked with developing the final constitution by the deadline of May 1996. These negotiations were a lot smoother than those for the Interim Constitution because the outline of the final document had already been hammered out and the agreed 'constitutional principles' dictated much of what would be possible in the final constitution.

Ramaphosa, Nelson Mandela, FW de Klerk and Roelf Meyer
during negotiations on the final constitution in 1996.
(Gallo Images/*Business Day*/Robert Botha)

By the time the drafters finalised the document, the relationship between the ANC and the NP in the Government of National Unity had become frayed. The final document, unsurprisingly, did not make provision for the continuation of this arrangement. South Africa would become a majoritarian state where the party that won an election would appoint the Cabinet and would govern using its majority in Parliament.

The consensus politics of the transition period was over, although there were substantial clauses in the Bill of Rights protecting individuals against an over-reaching state. The seeds were sown for a confrontation between the Constitution and political chauvinists, which would, perhaps inevitably, one day emerge.

*

Ramaphosa's enthusiasm for the Constitution was undimmed when I spoke to him about it twenty years later: 'I think the Constitution was the best, phenomenal achievement that, as a nation, we were able to have. It was the nation's birth certificate. It gave life to a brand-new democratic South Africa, and it gave birth to a nation. A nation that had a great father. The parentage was great – Nelson Mandela.' As far Ramaphosa was concerned, it was a 'balanced settlement': 'Nobody got 100 per cent of what they wanted, not the IFP, not the Democratic Party and the ANC. We didn't get 100 per cent, but we got most of what we thought would make up a democratic, non-racial South Africa. In our case, it was the foundation on which we would build, if you like, South Africa house.' What Ramaphosa returned to time and again was that the Constitution entrenched 'a human rights culture where there had been no human rights, respect, recognition or culture in our country. Just to entrench the Bill of Rights in the Constitution, interim as it was, was phenomenal.'

Some twenty years after its writing, the Constitution was beginning to be criticised for entrenching an order that was the result of a compromise between parties that was no longer relevant. The NP, which had held out for the protection of property rights and for safeguards against an aggressive redistributive state, was no more. It had gone into steep decline, and the rump of the party was eventually absorbed by the ANC.

Was a deal crafted decades ago still relevant? Ramaphosa's response to this question was: 'History actually required and dictated that it should be done in that way. There are still people who have this fantastic dream that we could have had it all. It could never have happened, so, in the end, the settlement we crafted was the best we could have and it behooves us to utilise it as a foundation, to utilise the levers that it gave us to advance further.'

In Ramaphosa's view, there was simply no alternative to a negotiated solution: 'The option could have been on the ANC's side, prosecute the struggle to total victory and march into Pretoria with guns blazing and on tanks and all that. Was that an option? It clearly was not an option. The apartheid regime could not have carried on in the same way. It clearly was a stalemate. We had a stalemate and out of the stalemate history – history! – decreed that we should build a nation out of the ashes of apartheid.'

Ramaphosa celebrates with Mandela after the signing of the final constitution
at Sharpeville Stadium on 10 December 1996. At far left is Frene Ginwala,
the Speaker of Parliament. (AAI Fotostock SA)

Ramaphosa describes the Constitution as 'a beachhead': 'We arrived on the beach and we could then go into the hinterland and achieve more, deepen democracy, extend a culture of human rights, begin the empowerment and the transformational project, stabilise the economy, make sure that our people get a better life and make sure you arrange the state in a way that it caters no longer for just a minority – two million people or so – but many more millions of people.'

The Constitution was only as good as the leadership that it empowered. In Nelson Mandela, South Africa had 'a good captain': 'He steadied this ship in stormy seas. He steadied it, and the project that Madiba took on of reconciliation and nation-building was so correct and its time had arrived. He was bold, he took risks and he was able to do the unprecedented – reach out to Afrikaners, make sure that [he continued to have support] on his constituency's side. He pacified people and got them to see the broader picture, the new South African picture. So, we've been very lucky. We should count our blessings, one by one. That's how lucky we've been.'

Ramaphosa would soon 'get lucky' in a very different way. When South Africa's white business oligarchs sought out potential empowerment partners to take up stakes in their sprawling conglomerates, his name would be at the top of the list. He was about to convert his political capital into real money.

FIVE

# *The commanding heights of business*

The banks were empowered, the advisers were empowered, the
merchant bankers, the lawyers and the accountants were all
empowered and the very people who were meant to be empowered
were not empowered and they ended up walking away with zero.
– *Cyril Ramaphosa*

When it became clear to Ramaphosa that he would not be rewarded with a senior Cabinet post after the promulgation of the
final Constitution in 1996, he surprised everyone by announcing
that he would be spearheading the ANC's deployment of cadres
'into business'.

Ramaphosa was no stranger to business, having run his own
construction outfit in Soweto when he was a much younger man.
And he had a grip like few others on South Africa's mining industry, having sat opposite mining bosses for many years during wage
negotiations as the representative of the NUM. He would soon
emerge as the driving force behind the first major 'black empowerment' deal of the post-apartheid era when he headed the consortium that bought a package of industrial assets held by Johnnic,
a subsidiary of Anglo American Corporation.[1]

The ANC's focus had been on the political settlement and the
creation of a stable, functioning democracy. Now it began to turn
its attention to economic transformation. Economic policy had
been driven by the limited redistributive thrust of the RDP, large
chunks of which had been borrowed wholesale from Cosatu. But

the RDP had focused more on how to allocate state resources to make up for the massive failure of the apartheid state to develop services, housing and infrastructure in black areas.

Business was a donor – Nelson Mandela would famously use his charisma to cajole big businesses into supporting development projects – and a participant in 'public-private' partnerships aimed at rolling out specific projects. But there was little coherent policy on how business itself could be made to become more representative of the country's demographics. The ownership of listed companies was heavily – almost exclusively – biased towards whites, a handful of whom dominated the Johannesburg Stock Exchange.

There had been initiatives to examine how black involvement in business could be bolstered. In 1992, two of these initiatives mirrored the rivalry between Mbeki and Ramaphosa. Mbeki organised a meeting at the Phinda Game Reserve, in KwaZulu-Natal, on the same weekend that the heads of the ANC's economic policy department, Trevor Manuel and Tito Mboweni, convened a black business summit at Mopane Lodge in the Kruger National Park. The Kruger summit was opened by Walter Sisulu and Ramaphosa. Mark Gevisser quotes an unnamed black businessman who said: 'It was either you were a Thabo Man and going to Phinda or a Cyril Man and going to Mopane. Some of us caucused, and we split up: "You go to Phinda and I'll go to Mopane." '[2]

The summits aside, the ANC remained unsure of what direction to take with business. Fearing that global markets would view South Africa as a socialist basket case, the party did its best to project itself as business-friendly. The end of the Cold War and the advent of the era of globalisation meant that socialists were very much on the back foot in economic policy discourse. Later, when he was Mandela's Trade and Industry minister, Trevor Manuel went out of his way to liberalise the trade environment, removing tariff protections and exposing local industries to global competition. But, with the new Constitution written and the pressure mounting to demonstrate decisive change in the economic sphere, attention began to turn to how business could be transformed.

South Africa's conglomerates, aware that the pressure was rising and, at the same time, that their inefficient, sprawling empires were out of touch with global competitors, began to look at unwinding some of their assets to black buyers. The problem was the absence of capital in the communities excluded by apartheid from the formal economy. Decades of economic exclusion had relegated black South Africans to roles on the margins of the economy – as manual workers, subsistence peasants or, at best, small businessmen. There were many black professionals, but their earnings were far inferior to those of whites and they were not able to accumulate sufficient savings to finance any serious intervention in the formal economy. There were some wealthy businessmen and civil servants in the former homelands, but they were the beneficiaries of apartheid patronage. Against tremendous odds and with great courage, a few entrepreneurs, such as Sam Motsuenyane, Herman Mashaba and Richard Maponya, had managed to build substantial businesses.

There was clearly a need to remove the structural constraints to establishing successful black-owned enterprises. In the years following the negotiated settlement, these constraints were largely eliminated – at least at the legislative level – by a succession of laws eliminating racial discrimination and setting out basic employment standards. The homelands had been abolished and the country's provincial boundaries redrawn, and for the first time all South Africans enjoyed the unfettered right to own property and to establish businesses wherever they wished. But the legislative changes did nothing to improve access to capital, which can take decades to accumulate in a community that has previously been excluded.

To solve the problem of access to capital and to respond to the mounting pressure for transformation, a cunning plan was hatched. The conglomerates would sell off parts of their businesses to black investors willing to gamble on the escalating value of shareholdings and on the payment of dividends being sufficient to pay off debt. And these stakes would be sold off at a substantial discount to their market value, annoying many of the existing shareholders. It was the dawn of the new black empowerment era, which would permanently reshape the business landscape.

*

Among the successful entrepreneurs interested in participating in this sort of purchase was Nthato Motlana. A Soweto community leader with a long struggle pedigree – he had been tried with Mandela during the Defiance Campaign in the 1950s – Motlana would come to be described as the 'father of black economic empowerment' after he formed New Africa Investments Limited (Nail) and bought a range of assets at discount prices as large companies sought empowerment partnerships. Motlana, who had made his way in business against the odds under oppressive conditions, was prickly about getting an empowerment handout. 'Don't talk to me about black empowerment because I don't come from that bloody genre. I come from a time when it was impossible and I did it. That's where I come from, not from some bloody political patronage,' he was quoted as saying in 1994.[3] His tune was about to change.

In 1995, while Ramaphosa was in the final stages of leading the drafting of the final Constitution, Motlana approached him about getting involved in a big move by Nail to acquire assets from Anglo American. He also approached Dikgang Moseneke – the future

Deputy Chief Justice – along with businessman Jonty Sandler, to explain his vision of a 'black Anglo American'.[4] Moseneke recalled: 'Dr Motlana explained that his dream team would also include Cyril Ramaphosa. At the time Cyril was a member of parliament and chairperson of the constituent assembly, which was entrusted with the duty to draft and adopt the final constitution. Jonty and Nthato had already held preliminary discussions with him and he had expressed his willingness to join the Nail executive team when his constitution-making obligations ended.'[5] Motlana wanted Ramaphosa to head up the new group's mining division, while Moseneke would run its financial services portfolio. Moseneke said he was offered 'an attractive remuneration package' that was the same as that being offered to Ramaphosa.

Just as the momentum for the big deal was building, and he had delivered the final Constitution, Ramaphosa announced that he was leaving politics to chart a way forward for black empowerment. The way he told it to me, he felt naturally drawn to a role in business: 'By and large we had just postponed our attention as the ANC on the economy, on the economic empowerment project and I felt that I would like to play a role in this. I think in part it was my own entrepreneurial spirit which I had had even before I had entered politics, years ago, which was surging to the fore.'[6]

He approached Mandela and the ANC with his plan and was granted permission. I asked him if it wasn't true that he was the victim of Machiavellian manoeuvring within the ANC that had shunted him out of politics: 'Not entirely true, not entirely true. Going into business was my choice. It was my choice. The one thing which I can say was that, soon after the constitution-making process, I wanted to revert back into the party and what piqued me was the continuous stories that now I was reverting back into the party to begin building my profile – building myself to have a go at challenging Thabo Mbeki.'

That, said Ramaphosa, was far from his mind: 'I had accepted that Thabo Mbeki was my leader, and, as a disciplined cadre of the ANC, I did not want to even be part of that. My view was that he had to execute the task he had been given by the party, finish that, and I was never one who wanted to undermine the leaders of the ANC who had a clear mandate and had been clearly elected by the organisation. With that type of story and view being spread around, it became a lot easier to then say: why don't I go to another frontier? The business frontier.'

Ramaphosa sat down with Mandela and discussed his plan. Then he discussed it with Mbeki. 'They both said: Ja, why don't we get you to go and pay attention to this?' Then it was discussed by the ANC national executive committee (NEC). 'So, I never felt that there was some Machiavellian plot or move on me. No. It was by choice.'

Mandela made the announcement to a surprised nation. Most had expected Ramaphosa to take a senior role in government. It was, said Ramaphosa, in the language of the ANC, 'deployment'. He said he had not planned to get involved in deal-making when he envisaged a role in business: 'The way it worked was that as soon as I got out of politics, my own original conception about going into business was much more sort of to build an NGO that was going to empower black people with a lot of training, capacity-building, enabling them to be able to operate effectively at the business level. And where we can open up opportunities for them and give them the tools which they would need to get going in business. That was my original thinking.'

Motlana, recognising the usefulness of an ANC heavyweight in his quest to secure an empowerment stake, came calling at just the right time. 'I was then corralled into playing a leading role in a consortium that was bidding for Johnnic,' said Ramaphosa.

Ramaphosa joined Nail's consortium, which wanted to buy the

Johnnic assets. These were heady days, and the consortium had no less than 73 participants at the outset. The Johnnic assets were part of the giant Anglo American Corporation, which dominated the Johannesburg Stock Exchange – and, indeed, the South African economy, with interests in mining, newspapers, breweries and food, among other sectors.

The move on Johnnic meant that Ramaphosa would once more encounter Harry Oppenheimer, the man he had berated ten years earlier, at the first anniversary celebrations of the *Weekly Mail*, when he was a trade unionist. This time they would talk business. 'I remember clearly going to see Mr Oppenheimer and saying: "Mr Oppenheimer, we are a group of 73 entities, we would like through this economic empowerment process to empower our black people to get into – to play a key role in – the economy,"' Ramaphosa recalled.

But he was to encounter his first major disappointment. You had to wonder if Oppenheimer remembered how Ramaphosa had humiliated him at their previous meeting. Coming as he did from the mineworkers' union, Ramaphosa had his eyes on Anglo's substantial mining assets, especially those in platinum, which were beginning their dramatic, decades-long bull run. Ramaphosa recalled the conversation:

'I remember him saying: "Yes, we are going to be selling our assets in Johnnic, but we are not going to sell our crown jewels."

'And I said: "What are those crown jewels?"

'And he said: "There is just no way, no way, we can give away or sell our platinum interests." And that was where the growth was.'

Instead of mining assets, the consortium was offered what Ramaphosa describes as 'medium-performing assets – the newspapers and the industrial sector, including Premier Foods and South African Breweries. And that was like the rump of what was being sold. But even that needed restructuring. Restructuring to a point where all you would finally end up with would be the news-papers and a bit of a stake in Times Media, which had a stake in-directly in MTN, which was still a young and growing asset.'

As the negotiations wore on, the number of entities in the con-sortium who could raise the money dropped from 73 to 23 – further evidence of the scarcity of capital and lack of black leverage. It was, to use Ramaphosa's description, 'a putative type of empower-ment in the sense that you were buying a stake in a company and relying on share performance and if the share did not perform you would walk away with nothing'. As it turned out, the 23 enti-ties would eventually walk away with very little because the shares did not perform: 'It was never real empowerment. All it really turned out to be was an opportunity to sit at the table and to vote and you never really owned the equity because the equity in the end relied on whether the share appreciated sufficiently so you could share in the upside.' The largest beneficiaries, according to Ramaphosa, were the banks: 'Those who financed the deal re-mained the true owners of the shares. The banks were empowered, the advisers were empowered, the merchant bankers, the lawyers and the accountants were all empowered and the very people who were meant to be empowered were not empowered and they ended up walking away with zero.'

Michael Spicer, who was on the other side of the table, told me that the Johnnic negotiation had been difficult: 'It was asymmet-rical – the commercial firepower of Anglo versus people with no experience. This really was uncharted territory. Memories of the violent bloody strike of '87 were fresh – 50 000 fired, dozens killed.'[7] What made the deal possible was the 'social capital' that had accumulated when Ramaphosa and Bobby Godsell had led the National Peace Accord process, a business-funded initiative to monitor potential incidents of political violence and then to pre-vent them by bringing political leaders together to find negotiated

Professor Wiseman Nkuhlu (left), Anglo American finance director
Mike King (centre) and Ramaphosa at the signing of the
landmark empowerment deal to acquire Johnnic in August 1996.
(Gallo Images/*Business Day*/Robert Botha)

solutions. This massive national effort to defuse political violence
opened the way for the Codesa talks.

Still, distrust remained. Anglo made a big effort to prevent the
ANC taking control of all its media assets. London's Pearson,
owners of the *Financial Times*, was persuaded to take a 50 per
cent stake in *Business Day* and the *Financial Mail*. Anglo's Argus
Group assets, including the *Cape Times*, *Cape Argus*, *The Star*
and *Pretoria News*, were sold to the Irishman Tony O'Reilly, own-
er of London's *Independent* newspaper, who renamed the group
Independent News and Media. Spicer reflected: 'In some ways,
we're a lot wiser now. We've all changed our views. I have no
doubt Anglo was pretty arrogant. We thought we knew it all.'

*

With the deal concluded, Ramaphosa oversaw the whittling-down of Johnnic. By 2005, Johnnic had sold off its interest in cellular network MTN and its market valuation had shrunk to just R1.7 billion.[8] It still possessed one sought-after asset: Tsogo Sun's money-spinning casinos in Gauteng province, including Montecasino. The casino assets were to become the subject of a bitter battle between Ramaphosa and Hosken Consolidated Investments (HCI), an investment company based in Cape Town. There was an added twist to the conflict: HCI's chairperson was Marcel Golding, once Ramaphosa's deputy at the NUM.

Golding and another trade unionist, Johnny Copelyn, had started HCI in 1997. By 2005, they had built it into an empowerment company with a valuation of R3.4 billion – exactly twice that of Johnnic. HCI had been buying Johnnic shares and made a bid to have Golding, Copelyn and HCI's executive director, Velaphi Mphande, elected to the Johnnic board. This had been blocked, ostensibly because of a conflict of interest. HCI's next move was to increase its shareholding in Johnnic to 40 per cent by buying a further 10 per cent holding from another gaming group. Black empowerment's first hostile takeover was under way.

Financial journalist Thebe Mabanga observed: 'By all accounts, it appears that a protégé, Marcel Golding, has outfoxed the master.'[9] By December 2005, the battle was over, and in January of the following year Ramaphosa stepped down as chairman of Johnnic, to be replaced by Copelyn.[10]

Under its new overlords, Johnnic announced it was paying out a dividend of R3 a share. HCI would get R244 million of that payout.[11] Reflecting on the takeover, Copelyn would later reject the 'cowboy' tag that had become attached to HCI: 'We were reluctant warriors. HCI always comes off looking like a bunch of cowboys, but in truth, I don't think we did more than aggressively defend ourselves against people trying to screw us into the ground.'[12]

Ramaphosa played down his defeat: 'Frankly speaking, I didn't have skin in the game. I just happened to be there when the skirmishes took place.'[13] Ramaphosa would eventually leave Nail after falling out with Sandler, taking his support staff with him.

Nail began to fall apart and it was soon hit by a new crisis over the payment of share options. Dikgang Moseneke found himself on the other side of the fence to Sandler and Motlana: 'When the share options were issued, they carried a rather modest value given the level of the Nail share price. The value of the executive share options rose through the roof.'[14] Moseneke and Zwelakhe Sisulu, who was also a Nail executive, thought the shares should not be paid out at the inflated price. Motlana and Sandler disagreed and left the company. By the time HCI took over Johnnic, Nail had long been delisted. Its assets had been sold off in 2001.

\*

The Johnnic experience was a steep learning curve. The initial empowerment model had a multiplier effect for a relatively small group of black businesspeople. Once they had their foot in the door, they acquired knowledge and greater access to capital and were then fancied when new deals were made. The mixture of political connectedness, access to money, membership of the business inner circle and growing understanding of how business worked made Ramaphosa and others who left the ANC for business, such as former Gauteng premier Tokyo Sexwale, former Mpumalanga premier Mathews Phosa and ANC executive member Saki Macozoma, the target of a succession of empowerment partnerships.

The result was that empowerment began to be criticised for rewarding what came to be called 'the same old faces' at the expense of the vast number of previously excluded black people, who remained on the margins of the economy. Ramaphosa told me: 'The only real empowerment came later, as we learned the ropes, as we deepened our knowledge and experience on how we could begin to run these companies through MTN, through TML [Times Media Ltd]. Then black people were given an opportunity, a real opportunity to get into the key management positions, and that spawned quite a lot of really outstanding executives because now they could be appointed by a board of directors consisting mainly of black people. That spawned really effective boards of directors, really effective black managers, financial directors, CEOs and we saw that flourishing through MTN which we had control of.'

Black management of MTN oversaw the broad-based Zakhele empowerment deal, which allowed workers at the company to participate in ownership. Recalled Ramaphosa: 'We saw MTN growing, and with MTN growing and becoming a global company, we saw key managers getting into top positions which, in a way, vindicated our entry into business.' Among those top managers was Phuthuma Nhleko, the MTN CEO and later its chairperson. Nhleko and Ramaphosa were to forge a lasting bond and they would continue to be involved in business together years later: 'It proved that if black people are given an opportunity, as good an opportunity as their white counterparts, they can actually demonstrate that they have the capabilities. That to me was the real outstanding achievement.'

When I asked Ramaphosa how he responded to criticism that the 'same old faces' were being empowered, he replied: 'The criticism is valid. In the beginning, it was the same old people as would happen in any situation. I guess in the United States, when they industrialised it was always the Rockefellers, the Fords, the Carnegies, and all that. That's what often happens with pioneers, people who will open the road, open the path, and soon thereafter, you had many more participants, even in the United States. The railroads were no longer just owned by the Rockefellers or the Carnegies. They were now owned by a plethora of people. This is what we are now seeing. It's no longer the same old people. It's now being spread more and more.' The new challenge, he said, was to build 'black industrialists' – 'black, serious businesspeople who will now lead top companies in manufacturing and a number of other disciplines. And that has a lot to do with education. As soon as we have more and more black people trained as accountants, as engineers, we will begin to see that happening. And that is coming. That is coming.'

In 1998, Thabo Mbeki appointed Ramaphosa to head a commission on black economic empowerment. It was to spend three years drafting policy. When it reported in 2001, the commission called on the state to play a more directly interventionist role to benefit the growth of black businesses and to realign procurement policy to encourage the emergence of more black companies. The commission proposed that each sector of business compile a voluntary 'charter' that would spell out empowerment goals. The first charter was developed for the fuel industry, the second for mining and the third for financial institutions.[15] The commission's report would lead to the passage of the Broad-Based Black Economic Empowerment Act 53 of 2003.

*

In 2001, Ramaphosa founded the Shanduka Group, described as a 'black-owned investment holding company'. Shanduka held stakes in a range of listed and unlisted companies in a breathtaking array of sectors – resources, food and beverages, financial services, energy, telecoms, property and industrial. The group operated in South Africa, Mozambique, Mauritius, Ghana and Nigeria.

Shanduka invested in three phases. It began as a purely financial investor. Then, if it liked what it saw, it moved on to 'acquire operating skills with a view to achieving significant influence in selected businesses'. In the final phase, it sought to gain operational control of what it viewed as 'long term core investments'.[16] The group had a claimed 'total black ownership' of 51 per cent, of which '18 per cent shareholding was held by broad-based trusts'.[17] Shanduka committed itself to spending R100 million on corporate social investment over ten years through vehicles such as the Adopt-a-School Foundation and Shanduka Black Umbrellas.

By the time Ramaphosa re-entered active politics in 2014, Shanduka was said be valued at some R8 billion, with his personal stake worth roughly R2.6 billion. In May 2014, Ramaphosa announced he would exit day-to-day involvement in business, and that he would disinvest from Shanduka Group in order to focus on his responsibilities as deputy president. In a statement issued by the Presidency, Ramaphosa said: 'Shanduka's majority shareholders have entered into an agreement that will, among other things, result in my complete divestment from the group. In the interim, my family's interests will be held in blind trusts. In the course of the next few weeks, I will take any further practical steps necessary to ensure that I comply with requirements of the Executive Ethics Code and uphold the integrity of my office.' The move, said Ramaphosa, had been made to 'remove the potential for any conflict of interest and enable me to effectively perform the functions of my position'.[18]

The plan, which appeared to have been approved by Shanduka's shareholders, was to merge their business interests in a giant new empowerment company, Phembani, which already held investments in Engen, BHP Billiton, Exxaro and AfriSam, with a book value of R13.5 billion. Ramaphosa had by then stepped down from the boards of several companies, including the Standard Bank Group and MTN, and had already resigned as executive chair-

person of Shanduka. Ramaphosa's replacement as chair of Shanduka was none other than his old comrade from the NUM, James
Motlatsi, who said, 'Cyril has left already and he will no longer
play a leading role within this company'.[19]

In July 2014, Ramaphosa was given a further four months to
complete his exit from businesses by President Jacob Zuma, whose
then spokesperson, Mac Maharaj, said: 'President Jacob Zuma
has agreed to a request by Deputy President Cyril Ramaphosa to
extend the period in which to dispose of any financial or business
interests that may give rise to a conflict of interest when perform-
ing his functions or place administration of such interests under
the control of an independent and professional person or agency.'[20]

By November, Ramaphosa had completed his withdrawal from
business. Shanduka announced: 'In effecting Mr Ramaphosa's exit,
Shanduka has disposed of certain assets in "non-regulated" sectors to Mr Ramaphosa. These include properties and McDonald's
South Africa. Shanduka Group will retain the bulk of its assets,
predominantly in resources and energy.' The statement said that
Shanduka's new shareholders were Mabindu Trust (49.5 per cent),
China Investment Corporation (33.6 per cent) and Standard Bank
(16.9 per cent).[21]

*

One of the companies Ramaphosa exited in 2014 gave him his
closest brush with the controversial Gupta family. In 1993, Eskom
had entered into a contract with a company called Optimum
Colliery, owned by the resources behemoth Billiton (later BHP
Billiton), to supply coal to the Hendrina power station in Mpumalanga for a 25-year period.[22] Until 2018, Optimum Colliery would
sell its coal to Eskom for R150 a ton, with agreed-on escalations
in the price. It was a long-term contract, and 25 years is a long
time in business. These escalations proved to be way below mining

inflation. By 2015, Optimum was still getting R150 a ton for its coal – well below the cost of producing it.

Perhaps unsurprisingly, the colliery changed hands several times. In 2008, it was sold to empowerment investor Eliphus Monkoe along with other assets. Monkoe's company bought another colliery and consolidated all the assets in a new company, Optimum Coal Holdings.[23] Ramaphosa came into the picture in 2012, when the Optimum assets were sold to Glencore, a multi-national mining and commodity trading company based in Switzerland. Ramaphosa's Shanduka Group became Glencore's empowerment partner.[24]

Glencore and Eskom were soon at each other's throats. Glencore was unhappy that the 25-year-old agreement forced it to sell coal to the power utility at below the price it could get elsewhere. In July 2013, the company wrote to Eskom, saying it would lose no less than R881 million that year due to the disadvantageous contract.[25] In May 2014 that year, the two parties signed a 'cooperation agreement' to explore ways of redoing the contract to make it more even-handed.

It was at this point that Ramaphosa, having become deputy president, announced he was exiting his empowerment stake in Glencore along with other business interests. He might have been out of the picture financially, but the events that followed would no doubt have left him open-mouthed with disbelief.

Former Transnet CEO Brian Molefe was appointed Eskom CEO in April 2015 and immediately set about undoing the cooperation agreement with Optimum, saying the utility would enforce the original contract. When Optimum countered with a request for a higher price, Molefe slapped the company with a R2.1 billion fine for supplying 'poor quality coal'.[26] The fine was eventually imposed in August, 'ironically in the same month in which it [Eskom] lifted the suspension on coal sourced for the Guptas' Brakfontein mine after it too had been found to be of poor quality', writes Pieter-Louis Myburgh in his excellent book, *The Republic of Gupta*.[27]

What exactly was Molefe up to?

Glencore faced having to close the mine due to the onerous fine. In the meantime, it began retrenching some 380 workers in an effort to cut costs. Two weeks after this decision, the Department of Mineral Resources, acting with unusual swiftness, suspended Optimum's mining licence because, by retrenching, it had not complied with labour law. As Ramaphosa watched from the sidelines, Optimum was placed under business rescue. It was faltering as a going concern and Eskom remained unmoved by its plight.

The reason for the pincer movement between Molefe and Eskom and the Department of Mineral Resources soon became apparent. The auditing firm KPMG made an appearance from the wings, approaching Glencore with an offer from an anonymous client willing to pay R2 billion for the struggling asset.[28] This was puzzling. Who would want to spend that amount of money on a firm that was facing a fine of R2.1 billion and was no longer an acceptable supplier to Eskom? There must have been one hell of an innovative business plan afoot. It turned out that KPMG was acting for the Gupta company Oakbay Resources & Energy.[29]

Glencore was not ready to sell and the negotiations with Eskom dragged on. Glencore had one hand tied behind its back: the coal-supply agreement dictated that Eskom would have to approve the sale of the coal mine.

Then an extraordinary thing happened. Eskom's head of procurement, Matshela Koko, entered the picture as Glencore finally became interested in selling the mine to Oakbay. During the negotiations between Eskom and Glencore over the sale of the coal mine, Koko made it plain that the utility would approve the sale only if the company's rights to export from the Richards Bay coal terminal and the Koornfontein coal mine were included.[30] It was all very odd. Why would Eskom get involved in negotiating a business transaction when its interests ended with the supply of coal from Optimum?

In September 2015, President Jacob Zuma appointed a new Mineral Resources minister, Mosebenzi Zwane. His predecessor, Ngoako Ramatlhodi, would later state publicly that he had been pushed out because he had refused to go along with favouring Gupta mining interests. Ramatlhodi said that he had been pressured to meet Molefe and Eskom chairman Ben Ngubane. At the meeting, they demanded that he suspend Glencore's mining licences.[31] The amaBhungane investigative journalism unit quoted Ramatlhodi as saying: 'They insisted that I must suspend all the Glencore mining licences pending the payment of the R2 billion . . . You must remember that the country was undergoing load-shedding at that time. I said to them: how many mines do these people have supplying Eskom? How many more outages are we going to have?'[32] He refused: 'I said I'm not going to shut the mines.'[33]

Zwane and the Guptas were tight. In previous administrative roles, Zwane had helped secure the highly irregular clearance for a plane carrying Gupta wedding guests to land at Waterkloof Air Force Base in April 2013. When he was MEC for Agriculture in the Free State, his department had sponsored a dairy farm project that had benefited the Guptas.[34]

Zwane's role soon became clear. He was the closer. 'In December 2015, about three months after taking up his new position at the [Department of Mineral Resources], Zwane travelled to Switzerland to meet with Ivan Glasenberg, Glencore's CEO,' writes Myburgh. The purpose of the meeting? To 'facilitate' the transfer of the Optimum assets from Glencore to Oakbay.[35] Zwane's spokesman said the minister was merely trying to 'engage stakeholders' to avoid job losses: 'Minister Zwane has committed himself to ensuring that his office has an open-door policy. This, in part, requires travelling to meet with all stakeholders to represent government's position on these pertinent matters. He will continue to do so.'[36]

A week later, the deal was made public. Eskom and Optimum went into arbitration over the R2.1 billion fine. Shortly before the arbitration hearing, Eskom said it had discovered a flaw in its quality control mechanism and the penalty was no longer justified. It agreed to settle the penalty at R300 million, effectively providing a R1.8 billion windfall for Optimum's new owners. This was not Eskom's first act of generosity to Optimum's new owners. It had already agreed to 'pre-pay' the company for future deliveries of coal.

To Ramaphosa, what occurred must have been astonishingly clear. As a former shareholder, he would no doubt have been kept abreast of the unfolding deal by his business network. What he saw was the Gupta state-capture Hydra in full mating regalia. Optimum was battered into submission by Eskom and the Department of Mineral Resources, and when it was on its knees, the minister entered the stage, *deus ex machina*, to close the deal in Switzerland.

Ramaphosa's eyes were now wide open.

*

By most measures, Ramaphosa succeeded spectacularly in business, building a multibillion-rand conglomerate out of the 'medium-performing assets' he could purchase at a discount from Johnnic. He served on the boards of countless listed companies – as many as 50, according to one report[37] – and emerged as a major force on the national business stage.

There was more than a little irony to this record of achievement. Twenty years after the advent of democracy, he had come full circle, adopting the conglomerate structure of the old-order businesses that had been broken up and sold off in empowerment deals. But there was a twist to the conglomerate model.

Empowerment firms were adopting the logic of big Afrikaner businesses such as PSG and Remgro. Rather than minority stakes, these companies now wanted a suite of businesses in which they had operational control.[38] And there was finally evidence that empowerment was spreading beyond the 'usual names' to involve a broader base of beneficiaries. Ramaphosa was certainly a key leader of this evolving model.

South Africa's Parliament requires MPs to declare their financial interests. Ramaphosa's declaration runs to three pages and gives a glimpse of the assets he accumulated during the 17 years he spent in business.[39] The register does not paint the full picture because it requires only the value of shares and 'other financial interests' to be stated. Other assets, such as those contained in trusts or properties, are not given a value. Nonetheless, the register paints a picture of someone who has built a fortune and invested it wisely.

Ramaphosa's biggest declaration in the 'Share and Other Financial Interests' section is of his 'game farming' – declared with the qualification 'Loan Account'. Ntaba Nyoni Estates is valued at some R120 735 000, making it one of the premier pieces of agricultural land in the country. A further R6 070 450 is declared for 'cattle farming' on Ntaba Nyoni. Compared to this, his other declared shareholdings – R3.5 million in Connaught plc, described as a 'UK investment' and R2.2 million in the paper firm Mondi Ltd – are trifling.

Ramaphosa declared 15 remaining 'directorships and partnerships', including several in 'meat abattoir' businesses under the Ramburg umbrella, his game farm, Puma sports cars and Micawber 799 and Micawber 800, which held his McDonald's restaurant interests. In addition, he declared ownership of 32 properties – either townhouses, flats or townhouses for retirement – and declared involvement in five trusts, listing himself as a 'beneficiary' in three of them: the Kruinpark Retirement Village Trust, Tshivhase Trust and the MCR Trust, with the latter bearing his initials.

*

Ramaphosa's game farm interests were to become the subject of headlines when one of the strangest controversies of post-apartheid South Africa occurred. In April 2012, when a buffalo cow called Tanzania, with very impressive horns (the span of a buffalo's horns is apparently an important measure of its value), and its calf came up for auction, Ramaphosa got sucked into a bidding war. When the price reached somewhere over R18 million, Ramaphosa acknowledged defeat and withdrew from the bidding, probably thinking that was that. The cow and calf were sold for R20 million to one Jaco Troskie. The seller burst into tears of joy. Troskie was philosophical about how much he was spending: 'When the cow has four calves, I will already have got my money back,' he said.[40] It was a business decision he was prepared to stand by. Little did Ramaphosa know that he would become the object of vicious criticism for attempting to spend millions on game animals while the workers at the Lonmin platinum mine, in which he had a substantial shareholding, were up in arms over low pay.

Leading the criticism was Julius Malema, formerly the firebrand head of the ANC Youth League, who had founded a new party, the Economic Freedom Fighters (EFF), following his expulsion from the ANC. The relationship between Ramaphosa and Malema was coloured largely by the fact that it was Ramaphosa who had presided over the disciplinary hearing that had led to Malema's expulsion from the party. (This episode is covered in more detail in Chapter 6.) In a 'Letter from the Commander in Chief' (Malema's title in the EFF), Malema later wrote: 'The characteristics that defined the "Boers" are the same characteristics that define Cyril

Ramaphosa today, one who is not afraid to go [and] bid to buy an animal for R18 million, and one who is possibly complicit in the massacre of Mineworkers in Marikana, but will use State institutions to exonerate himself.'[41]

In one of the stranger political moments of recent times, Ramaphosa, realising he was on a losing wicket, chose to apologise for his losing bid. The ANC's December conference (held in Mangaung) was approaching and he was taking no chances. He told radio station SAfm: 'Yes, I did put a bid and that was a mistake on my part. It was a mistake. I regret it. It was a mistake to even put up my hand to do so . . . I've been chastised by some of my good comrades, and even before they chastised me, I did admit that was a mistake. I regret it because it is an excessive price in the sea of poverty. I belong to a community and it was one of those moments when I was blind-sided.'[42]

It was an extraordinary public statement. After all, Ramaphosa had been bidding on a business asset, not a personal luxury. He recognised that the emotional response of ordinary people would be incomprehension and he decided to avoid the controversy altogether. It was all the more extraordinary because white businessmen, who had made their money under apartheid, were not subject to the same standard. Barely a year later, Afrikaner mogul Johann Rupert was part of a group of investors that spent R40 million on a bull. 'It is a very special bull, arguably the best bull in SA. Lots of breeders tried to buy it,' said Rupert.[43] There was no controversy. Apparently, a different standard applied to Ramaphosa, who was supposed to consider the possible political fallout that might result from his agricultural purchases.

Ramaphosa would talk about his farming in an interview with *Farmer's Weekly* magazine in May 2012: 'I have been a cattle farmer for quite a while. I farm with what other people call "exotic" cattle: Boran from Kenya, Ankole from Uganda and Bonsmara.

My Bonsmara and my Boran are stud, and the Ankole are a breed under consideration by the Department of Agriculture. I've always had a deep love for farming, and that's how I got into game breeding.' He continued: 'I have some common species of game on my farm, and when I realised that the game industry was beginning to boom, I decided to enter into the more "exotic" side of things. First and foremost because it is an investment, secondly because it is farming, and thirdly because it is a wonderful contribution to conservation.'[44]

Finally, he turned to the auction of the buffalo cow and calf: 'Well, what we have seen is that there has been a continuous and sustained growth in the industry. A buffalo cow such as Tanzania that fetched R20 million comes once in a lifetime, or as the auctioneer said, "once in a millennium". I don't think you will see cows like that popping up all over the show.'[45] Ramaphosa had clearly taken to farm life. 'I've made many Afrikaans friends. I'm finding that there's a lot of commitment to change and to securing a common future for the industry, where all those who have been excluded historically will be included. That to me is quite comforting.'[46] Five years later, Ramaphosa would sell one of his Ankole bulls for R640 000,[47] with no public criticism. Apparently, it was okay to make a lot of money from game farming, but not okay to spend a lot.

*

He amassed a fortune, but was his heart really in it? Michael Spicer's view is that Ramaphosa's sojourn in business was an act of exile from his real passion: politics: 'He exiled himself. I never had any doubt that what makes his blood pump is politics. Business was a means to an end, I'm 100 per cent certain of that.'

Spicer's take on Ramaphosa's legacy is not as flattering as most: 'He accumulated a lot of wealth. It's not that he wasn't a particularly astute businessman. These things dropped into his lap. Take McDonald's, for example. They wanted a politically connected partner and he found himself in the fast-food business. One of the reasons some of my colleagues like him is that he talks the corporatist language.' Ramaphosa was most comfortable with the deal-making politics of big business and labour at the National Economic Development and Labour Council (Nedlac).

Ramaphosa's decision to return to politics was perhaps inevitable. But there would be one final chapter to his business career that would pose serious questions about his judgement.

Among the companies that Shanduka acquired a stake in was a marginal platinum producer called Lonmin. Ramaphosa was appointed to its board. The company's struggle to survive against growing wage demands and a falling platinum price would create the conditions for a perfect storm, one that would rock Ramaphosa's credibility to its very foundations.

A dusty koppie near the small North West town of Marikana was about to become the scene of post-apartheid South Africa's greatest tragedy.

# SIX
## *The depths of Marikana*

I take full responsibility of my role in it, and once again, my role was as follows. I was disturbed upon hearing the news that 10 miners, 10 innocent miners, had been killed. My reaction was: this cannot be activism. This is a criminal act. Back then I felt that the situation should be dealt with by the law. It was inappropriate language. I cannot try to be smart about it. – *Cyril Ramaphosa*

Ramaphosa's stellar business career represented a high point in his life. But, before he left business for politics, one of his business associations would lead to a low point, perhaps even the lowest point of his life.

On 16 August 2012, members of the police opened fire on striking mineworkers at a platinum mine near Marikana, close to Rustenburg in the North West province. By the time the shooting stopped, 34 mineworkers were dead and a further 70 were wounded.

The Marikana mine was owned by the UK's Lonmin plc. Ramaphosa served as a non-executive director on its board. Ramaphosa's company, Shanduka, held a 50 per cent stake in Incwala Resources, a black economic empowerment company that, in turn, held 18 per cent of two Lonmin subsidiaries – Western Platinum and Eastern Platinum. Shanduka effectively held a 9 per cent stake in Lonmin. Ramaphosa's investment in Lonmin had not paid back handsomely. On the contrary, while Incwala was worth around US\$600 million in 2010, when Ramaphosa bought his stake, it had plummeted to around US\$398 million by September 2012.[1] The decline in the company's share price had been under way for more than a year by the time of the Marikana events.

The shooting of the mineworkers at Marikana shocked South Africa to its core. It had previously been unthinkable that the police service of a post-apartheid government would use live ammunition against striking workers. It was a disaster that closely resembled the atrocities perpetrated by the apartheid government, events such as the Sharpeville massacre of 1960 and the repression of the Soweto student uprising of 16 June 1976.

The incident was to present Ramaphosa with the biggest challenge of his political career, after politically charged allegations were levelled against him over emails and other communication he had had with Lonmin and government ministers before the shootings. So, was Ramaphosa guilty of intervening in a manner that caused the police to shoot the strikers down, as has been alleged? The allegation was exhaustively dealt with by the commission of inquiry into the incident, headed by retired judge Ian Farlam.

The air at the Farlam Commission was thick with politics. Leading the assault against Ramaphosa was lawyer Dali Mpofu, who represented the families of some who had died at Marikana. But Mpofu was also a member of the leadership of the EFF, alongside Julius Malema. Malema had been expelled from the ANC after the findings of the disciplinary panel led by Ramaphosa. It was clear that the EFF was gunning for Ramaphosa. Did they have grounds to do so? The answers are contained in the commission's findings.

\*

The Farlam Commission submitted its final report, entitled 'The Marikana Commission of Inquiry: Report on matters of public, national and international concern arising out of the tragic incidents at the Lonmin mine in Marikana, in the North West Province', to President Jacob Zuma on 31 March 2015 – some two and a half years after the event. The commission's terms of reference were broad and included the events in the days leading up to the shooting. Lonmin's conduct fell squarely within the terms of reference, including 'whether it exercised its best endeavours to resolve any dispute/s which may have arisen (industrial or otherwise) between Lonmin and its labour force on the one hand and generally among its labour force on the other'. The commission would also investigate whether Lonmin had 'by act or omission' increased labour tensions or 'directly or indirectly caused loss of life or damage to persons or property.'[2]

The terms of reference also included the following clause: 'The conduct of individuals and loose groupings in fomenting and/or otherwise promoting a situation of conflict and confrontation which may have given rise to the tragic incident, whether directly or indirectly.' Ramaphosa's name was to feature prominently among those 'individuals' whose conduct was to be examined because, as a non-executive director, he had communicated with Lonmin management and with government officials on the days leading up to the shooting.

The background to the Lonmin strike had its own connection with Ramaphosa. The NUM, which he had been instrumental in turning into the country's foremost trade union, had entered into decline as the mining industry had faltered and other, more aggressively populist, unions had begun to challenge its hold on the workers. One of these was the Association of Mineworkers and Construction Union (Amcu), led by Joseph Mathunjwa. Amcu had been formed in 1998 as a breakaway from the NUM. It styled itself as 'apolitical and non-communist'.[3]

The dispute that precipitated the violent confrontation at Marikana was the direct result of the failure of the NUM to gain the confidence of some workers, who regarded the union as an unreliable representative of their interests. The NUM had been challenged by Amcu, but had remained the recognised majority union at Lonmin, and had, a year or so before, reached a multiyear agree-

ment with management on wages and other conditions of employment. Testifying before the commission, NUM national office bearer
Erick Gcilitshana had told of the painstaking process followed
by the NUM in concluding the agreement. Mass meetings, report-
backs, final mandates, branch meetings with shop stewards and
a range of other gatherings were held to properly consult with
workers.

By now the NUM followed a well-worn, professional process. The
commission described this in detail, including how '[t]he demands
are first forwarded to a dedicated market research section within
NUM's head office, where they are assessed for consistency with
the union's policies and evaluated against industry and market
norms and practices'. Gcilitshana said this was done 'to ensure
that NUM does not make unreasonable demands of the employers
and in turn, that it does not create unreasonable expectations'.

Such a system works in an environment where there is predict-
ability, one where agreements are hammered out and then complied with diligently by all parties. But when a party to such an
agreement unilaterally changes the rules of the game and goes
rogue, all the rules begin to be challenged and the game changes
into one where power confronts power. That is exactly what occurred at Lonmin's neighbouring Implats mine.

On 18 December 2011, the management at Implats made a
calamitous decision to grant an additional wage increase of 18 per
cent to a certain category of its workers. As the commission noted:
'This decision by Implats, according to the evidence, put NUM
in a spot.' The term 'spot' was a great understatement. What
occurred immediately was that the collective agreement was
totally undermined.

NUM members were angry. For one thing, the increase applied
to some workers and not others. For another, it created the
impression that the NUM leadership and their 'dedicated market

research section' had lied when they had persuaded workers to accept the deal because the owners' 'coffers have been exhausted'. From that point on, the NUM's influence over the angry workers diminished sharply and it came to be seen, alongside management, as the enemy.

In a little-examined prequel to the Marikana showdown, in October 2011 rock drill operators at Implats embarked on an unprotected strike that was, in the words of the commission, 'characterized by high levels of violence and intimidation much of which was directed at the NUM and its members'. By the time the Implats strike ended, in April 2012, four people had lost their lives and 60 had been injured. The NUM offices at Implats were forcibly closed and Implats dismissed 17 200 workers, most of whom it later re-employed. It is a mark of how inured South African journalists and the reading public are to violent labour unrest that these events were barely reported on at all.

The parallels between the Implats strike and the Lonmin strike were many. Both involved rock drill operators; both were preceded by demands outside the normal collective bargaining structures; both strikes were unprotected; and both were 'accompanied by high levels of violence and intimidation'. Significantly, 'in both strikes, the NUM offices were threatened and targeted; both strikes resulted in NUM losing membership and Amcu gaining membership'.

What was unfolding before Ramaphosa's eyes was the decline of the NUM as populist demands for wage improvements gained traction with workers outside of the painstakingly constructed 'official channels' where collective bargaining was supposed to take place. From then on, the conflict at Lonmin escalated steadily and the events that would draw Ramaphosa into the drama began to unfold.

\*

On the morning of Thursday 9 August 2012 – a public holiday celebrating women – as many as 3 000 rock drill operators gathered at Marikana's Wonderkop Stadium. They had rejected special allowances offered by Lonmin and decided to embark on an illegal strike – unprotected, in the jargon of the law – to demand a monthly salary for their category of worker of R12 500. They marched on the offices of Lonmin's Platinum Division.

The workers had made a perilous decision. Instead of following the established path of approaching their union representatives to take up their demands, they would go it alone, representing themselves. It was another crushing blow to the union that had once been held in such high regard. To some extent, the NUM was to blame for its inflexibility. It had previously been approached and had said it would not take the drillers' demands forward. As far back as 2006, the union had been asked to intervene and had failed to respond to the request, according to the testimony of some before the Farlam Commission.

Now worker anger boiled over and they chose the NUM as their target. Not only had the union failed to take forward their demands, but it had also, in the words of the commission, 'actively assisted workers to go to work during the night, which constituted actions aimed at breaking the strike that the protesters were trying to enforce'. Striking workers marched on the NUM offices. This resulted in a bloody confrontation, with two strikers dying.

The NUM would later explain to the commission that its officials had fired in self-defence, and that 'the shooting in fact saved the lives of some 20 to 30 of them from the crowd of approximately 3 000 persons converging on them. They maintain that it was the strikers who threw stones at them first.' The NUM explanation did not hold water with the strikers, who prepared to retaliate. They called in a sangoma, who arrived after dark. Bare-chested strikers presented themselves to the sangoma one by one and rituals were performed. These rituals were apparently to make the strikers impervious to bullets fired at them.

A man, described by the commission as 'a member of Lonmin Security', who had infiltrated the crowd of strikers would testify that he had witnessed them saying they would not sleep that night as they had to prepare their retaliation for those killed during the march: 'When I arrived back at my JOC [joint operational centre] team, I reported what I had witnessed. I mentioned that the Sangoma was present and had promised the crowd that if they participated in his rituals they would not need to fear the firearms of their enemies because the firearms would either jam or the bullets would turn to water before striking them. I am not sure whether my superiors took my recommendations seriously due to the fact that they laughed regarding the water bullet issue', he testified.

The following day, the confrontation ratcheted up a notch. Dewald Louw, a Lonmin security officer, would describe the strikers on the morning of 12 August 2012 as 'militaristic, organised and disciplined'. According to Louw, their body language was 'hostile and attacking, especially the manner in which they gestured with their spears'. The commission heard that one of the strikers moved his spear across his throat 'conveying a message that they were going to slaughter him'.

It was to be a violent day.

Two security officers – Mr Mabelani and Mr Fundi – were killed and their shotguns taken. Two vehicles were set alight. A Murray & Roberts employee saw a Mr Madebe lying on the ground and 'realized that this person had been chopped in his face and he was lying between the burning cars'. The commission concluded: 'It is clear from the evidence that there was simply no adequate SAPS presence at any of the events that occurred on the 12th. This is not disputed by SAPS.'

The following day, 13 August 2012, Julius Langa – a production team leader – was 'brutally killed'. The commission reported: 'According to the post-mortem report Mr Langa had 18 incised wounds on his chest, back and upper limbs. These wounds varied from 1cm to 11cm. He also had wounds on his face and head.' He had been stabbed with pangas and knives. 'The evidence before the Commission is overwhelming that Mr Langa was killed by strikers on his way to work', the report continued. 'According to Mrs Langa, the last time she saw her husband was when he left for work in the early hours.'

Five more would die that day, two of them policemen – Warrant Officers Monene and Lepaaku – and three of them strikers – Mr Mati, Mr Jokanisi and Mr Sokanyile.

Policing strategies appeared to be chaotic and ineffective. At one point, Major General William Mpembe tried to persuade the strikers to hand over their weapons, saying he was counting to ten. When he got to three, the strikers had already moved through the police line. At another point, a teargas canister was fired at strikers who were being escorted by the police, triggering a fight between police and strikers. No one was ever have found to have given the order that teargas be fired. General Mpembe denied giving the order even after a Captain Thupe said: 'General, I heard you give the order.'

Captain Thupe's testimony suggested that the police fired at least 37 live rounds at the strikers. Police commanders are expected to compile a 'shooting list' that details who fired, how many rounds they fired and which weapons they used. Thupe's shooting list recorded that three policemen, including himself, had opened fire with hardened ammunition, one with a pistol and two with R5 automatic rifles.

Thupe's vivid description of how the police ran from the strikers, throwing stun grenades, until he was attacked from behind and stabbed in the chest with knives and assegais before being saved by the driver of a Nyala armoured vehicle, reads like a description from a war zone and provides a chilling foretaste of the havoc to come.

Striking Lonmin workers on Wonderkop at Marikana, outside Rustenburg, on 15 August 2012. (Greg Marinovich/South Photographs/Africa Media Online)

Police began to formulate a plan aimed at bringing order to what had become a battlefield. The outline of the plan was that the strikers, who were gathering on a low koppie, would be 'encircled' and then processed through a line of police officers who would confiscate their weapons as they exited the koppie area. Exactly how this would be done was mapped out in some detail. A barbed-wire cordon would be drawn around the koppie by police vehicles equipped to release the fencing as they moved forward. The fencing would be uncoiled in two directions around the koppie at the same time 'to ensure that the encirclement took place quickly'. A 'filtering line' of police Nyalas would be placed between the koppie and an informal settlement that was seen as the destination of the strikers. Those arrested – presumably because they had been involved in offences earlier in the week – would be dealt with at a 'processing zone' after the operation.

On the morning of Tuesday 14 August, another body was found at the back of the koppie. It was that of Isaiah Twala, a Lonmin supervisor. Twala and Christopher Malinga had gone to meet striking workers at the koppie. It is not clear why they did this. They may have been attempting to talk to them or to gather information. In any event, it ended badly. When the two men decided to leave, they were confronted by two men wearing blankets and carrying sharp instruments. They were made to sit in the middle of a group of 12 men and were questioned. Twala was accused of being an *impimpi* (informer). He was escorted to the 'other side of the mountain'. 'Later [Malinga] heard the sound of two gun shots coming from that direction', the report said. 'Later, the same persons that had left with Mr Twala returned but Mr Twala was not with them.'

Malinga recalled a chilling detail. One of the men who had taken Twala to the other side of the mountain returned and began cleaning his panga by wiping the blade on the grass. Malinga realised that he was cleaning blood from it. The commission concluded: 'As is apparent from the aforegoing, it would appear as if Mr Twala was killed, execution style, by a number of strikers, apparently acting in concert, because of a suspicion that he was spying on them on behalf of their employer and/or NUM.'

That morning, an attempt was made to negotiate with strikers about leaving the koppie. Lonmin's position remained that it would not talk to the striking workers outside organised bargaining structures. The police 'encirclement plan' was explained by Lieutenant General Zukiswa Mbombo, the SAPS provincial commissioner. She said police would 'circle' the workers and then talk to them to give them an opportunity to lay down their weapons and leave the koppie one by one.

Then came the comment that was to be the subject of much shock when it became known after the shootings. If the workers did not lay down their weapons, 'it is blood' she said. Asked to explain this statement by the commission, she said she meant that if the strikers did not surrender, there would be injury or death.

There can be no denying these words as they were recorded. In the transcript, she takes a telephone call from the national police commissioner, Riah Phiyega, and can be heard saying, '[T]here are about 500 to 1 000 that are there. So are we are thinking that whilst they are at that number, we can maybe circle them around . . .'

The police were building up their forces. On Monday, there were 209 members, on Tuesday 532 members, and by Wednesday 689 members were available for deployment.

Mbombo's testimony would also draw Ramaphosa into the mounting conflict. She testified that she had spoken to the Minister of Police, Nathi Mthethwa, who had said Ramaphosa was calling him and 'pressurising' him. She said that she had been asked by the commissioner who the shareholders of Lonmin were. When she replied that she did not know but that the minister had mentioned Ramaphosa, Phiyega had replied that she now 'got it'.

Mbombo explained further, giving her take on the political context. The commission reported: 'Lieutenant General Mbombo referred to the fact that Mr Ramaphosa had presided over the hearing of the appeal brought by Mr Julius Malema against the decision of the African National Congress to expel him from the party and that Mr Ramaphosa was, as she put it, "very strong in terms of the decision made". She went on to mention that Mr Malema had intervened in the dispute at Impala and that the police had been able to manage the situation there after his visit.

She stated that in her discussions with the National Commissioner they had been concerned about the fact that if once again it came across that Mr Malema had defused the situation it would seem as if he has taken charge of the mines. She added that because of Mr Malema's known position that the mines should be nationalised it had "a serious political connotation" that had to be taken into account . . .'

The commission found that Ramaphosa's call to Mthethwa had influenced Mbombo's decision-making at Marikana, and that she had taken 'into account irrelevant political considerations' in approaching the situation, specifically:

1. She did not want mining companies to be seen to be supporting Amcu;
2. She did not want mining companies to undermine NUM;
3. She was responding to what she perceived as pressure from Mr Cyril Ramaphosa whom she considered to be politically influential;
4. She wanted to end the violence before Mr Julius Malema arrived in Marikana and was given credit for defusing the situation;
5. She was concerned to put an end to a situation where an opposition member of Parliament was involving himself in the community.

Later, when Mbombo was cross-examined by the evidence leaders, '[s]he was unable to provide an adequate explanation for her denial that the . . . inferences listed above can validly be drawn . . .' What was clear was that the commissioner had introduced political factors into the decision-making around Marikana, which the Farlam report found was 'inconsistent with our constitutional and statutory regime which requires that policing be conducted in an impartial and unbiased manner'.

On the morning of Wednesday 15 August 2012 – the day before the mass shooting – the police met with officials of the NUM. The union wanted the strikers to be disarmed. Major General Mpembe replied: 'I need to do my job and you also tell me to remove firearms . . . I cannot go there and disarm people. It would be bloodshed . . . I need to go in a specific house [and] disarm them. That is the only way.' This analysis by a senior policeman made a simple point: it would be foolish and lead to 'bloodshed' to attempt to disarm the strikers en masse. It would have been much more sensible to employ normal policing methods – identifying suspects, visiting them individually at their homes and dealing with crimes.

Tragically, this moment of common sense would be swept aside by the police leadership. The commission agreed with the argument of the evidence leaders that 'Major General Mpembe clearly foresaw bloodshed if the police went in to disarm and disperse the strikers and he was realistic in that regard. Despite this foresight SAPS moved to the tactical phase without putting in place any substantive measures to mitigate against bloodshed and the loss of life. The SAPS leadership appeared to have reconciled itself to the notion that bloodshed was a real possibility, if not an inevitability.'

The decision to encircle and forcibly remove the strikers from the koppie was not taken by tactical commanders on the ground but rather by Lieutenant General Mbombo with the support of the SAPS leadership. The decision was taken at an extraordinary session of the police leadership on the evening of 15 August at which the national commissioner, provincial commissioners and other senior intelligence and operational leaders were present. The commission said it was disturbed by the fact that the police had withheld information about this meeting from it, as it was evidence that the decision to go to the 'tactical option' had been taken the day before and not in the heat of the moment.

*

By the morning of Thursday 16 August 2012, the police deployment had swelled to 718 members and the 'tactical option' was set in stone. That morning, Mbombo addressed a press conference. A transcript reads: 'I'm saying we are ending the strike today . . . What I told you is today we are ending this matter.'

The tragic events would play out in two theatres, 'Scene One' and 'Scene Two' in the language of the commission. At 'Scene One', 16 people would die in a fusillade of police gunfire.

There was, on the part of the police, a great deal of operational confusion. Stun grenades, teargas canisters and water cannon were fired. Non-lethal force, the commission found, was used later than it ought to have been, and when it was used, it had the effect of driving strikers towards the police line: 'All the teargas and stun grenades fired before the shootings were fired behind the leading group of strikers with the result that if they tried to move away from the teargas canisters and stun grenades they would have moved towards the TRT [tactical response team] line.'

There was some evidence that the strikers were preparing for a bloody showdown. Lieutenant Colonel Stephen McIntosh, a trained hostage negotiator, testified that a Mr Noki approached a Nyala, asking the police to sign a piece of paper that stated '[W]e are going to kill each other today'. The man went on to warn that 'these hippos would not leave this place and you will all die today'.

A Mr Ntsenyeho delivered a speech within earshot of the police in which he is said to have stated: 'We said that we would leave here, after getting the money we want. Otherwise, we will die on this mountain. None of us will be expelled, none of us will leave whilst we are here. We would rather die. There is no way that Lonmin can hire people while we are here. Otherwise, Lonmin must close. It must be finished with Lonmin, if it is finished with us. I am finished.' But such militant and provocative rhetoric is frequently used at South African political and union gatherings and very seldom translates into actual violent action. The police perhaps recalled these speeches afterwards when they were reaching for justification for the shootings. What is notable is that Ntsenyeho was shot through the neck and thigh with R5 bullets. He died towards the back of the pile of bodies at Scene One.

The commission pointed out that Ntsenyeho approached the kraal unarmed, which hardly suggests he intended to attack the heavily armed SAPS members. His shooting appears more in keeping with a view that the police targeted troublemakers and shot them down, regardless of their proximity to their firing line.

No fewer than 328 rounds of live ammunition were fired at 'Scene One' over the course of 12 seconds or less. Even if the strikers had posed a threat, the commission observed, 'It is apparent from the video material that three strikers fell in the first three seconds of the volley and thus after that stage no conceivable threat existed.' Yet the police kept firing. Gary White, a policing expert who testified, said: 'A large number of the shots continued to be fired into what was essentially a dust cloud without sight of any specific target.'

After the machine guns had rattled for nine seconds, Captain Loest raised his fist in the air and shouted, 'Cease fire!' The gory results of the firing were now plain to see. The commission's account provides gruesome but essential reading: 'The evidence indicates that R5 bullets tend to disintegrate when entering the body of a victim. This is what happened at Marikana. As a result, it is not possible on the ballistic evidence to connect any member who shot at Marikana with any person who died.'

For more than an hour, the wounded lay moaning in agony without medical attention, adding the crime of gross neglect to murder. 'In view of the fact that it was foreseen that four hearses were required and four thousand extra rounds of ammunition was ordered, the question arises as to whether in the planning of the operation arrangements were made for sufficient medical personnel to attend,' the commission observed.

At 'Scene Two', about 500 metres away, 14 more strikers would die, many shot in cold blood and with what appears to have been the same murderous intent. In total, 34 would die at the hands of the police that day.

*

Once the smoke and dust had settled and the blood had begun to soak away, news of the shooting spread quickly across the country and around the world. The reaction was one of horror. It seemed impossible to believe that the promise of a democratic, inclusive South Africa could be so dishonoured. More shocking was the obvious parallel between this brutal police shooting and the killings committed in the name of apartheid.

But the condemnation of the killing was not universal. On the day after the shooting, national commissioner Riah Phiyega addressed a parade of SAPS members. Her words demonstrated a shocking lack of awareness and empathy: 'I come before you to actually say, trying as it may be, mourning as we are, let us take note of the fact that whatever happened represents the best of responsible policing. You did what you did, because you were being responsible, you were making sure that you continued to live your oath of ensuring that South Africans are safe, and that you equally are a citizen of this country and safety starts with you.'

The commission observed with cutting understatement: 'When one bears in mind that the statement was made on the day after 34 civilians had been killed by members of the SAPS and the President announced that a Commission of Inquiry would be established, the statement that "whatever happened represents the best possible policing" was singularly inappropriate because it set out what was from then on to be the official police line: that no blame at all attached to the police for what happened because they had been responsible in doing what they did. This was calculated to effect a closing of the ranks, encouraging those who had participated in the operation to withhold contrary information from the Commission and indeed to deny that mistakes had been made and things had been done that could not be described as "the best of possible policing".'

Phiyega was not alone. Also speaking at the parade was Police minister Nathi Mthethwa. His words were equally devoid of sensitivity to the horror that had occurred: 'You must know that as your Minister and on behalf of the Government, the Executive as a whole, on behalf of the President of the Republic, Commander in Chief of all the armed forces in this country, we are all behind you.' Such chauvinist assertions of bravado cemented the public view that the authorities intended to kill the strikers in a show of power.

Even an officer who had led the forces on the ground appeared unaware of the effect of the massacre. Brigadier Adriaan Calitz briefed members at the parade, saying: 'At this stage we did nothing wrong. From the planning to the execution was 110 per cent. Exactly how we plan it and it is not often that this happens in this large group. I have to congratulate you. Exactly how we planned it and we briefed the commanders, exactly we executed in that line.' Just in case any members present doubted their actions were justified, he added: 'Nothing, nothing, nothing was wrong. Okay? You acted? It was justified and that is exactly the commitment and cooperation that we are going to give the people.'

The effect of these ill-considered statements was to increase the political pressure on the government, and, unsurprisingly, Ramaphosa was soon drawn into the controversy.

*

What was Ramaphosa's role in the events at Marikana? Did he egg the government on to act with violence against the strikers? Had he abandoned his lifelong humanism and concern for workers in favour of a more arrogant – even violent – attitude to defend his business interests?

Driven by Julius Malema, this narrative soon gained momentum. Ramaphosa's reputation suffered its greatest damage, even as he was planning a return to the political stage. With the ANC's Mangaung conference approaching in December, there was already talk that he had been offered the deputy presidency on Jacob Zuma's slate, and his political foes fell on the Marikana events like hyenas.

So prominent was the criticism of Ramaphosa that the Farlam Commission devoted an entire chapter of its report (Chapter 19: Mr Cyril Ramaphosa) to his role in the incident. The chapter began with an outline of the links between Ramaphosa and Marikana. Ramaphosa had exchanged emails with Lonmin personnel between 11 and 15 August 2012: 'They recorded that Mr Ramaphosa had conversations relating to the events at Marikana which are being investigated by the Commission with the then Minister of Police Mr Nathi Mthethwa and with the Minister of Mineral Resources, Ms Susan Shabangu.'

Advocate Dali Mpofu, counsel for the injured and arrested persons, seized on a phrase used by Ramaphosa in an email encouraging a more effective security force response to the strike. Ramaphosa had described the strikers as criminals and had called for 'concomitant action' to be taken. Mpofu argued that the emails were evidence of 'concerted pressure that was being put, among others, on the police – well firstly on the government not to call the strike a strike or not to call it labour related but to call it so-called criminal action and that was a platform from which it would be easier to inflict violence on strikers.' The essence of the argument was that there was a causal connection between Ramaphosa's statements and the killing of strikers by police.

Mpofu argued that Ramaphosa's intervention 'triggered a series of events which determined the timing of the massacre. He knew exactly what he was doing and he is the cause of the Marikana massacre, as we know it. It was demonstrated that he has a case to answer on 34 counts of murder and many counts of attempted murder as well as intent to do grievous bodily harm.'

Ramaphosa's response was to argue that he had not anticipated that the police would shoot the strikers, and that he certainly did not support this action, which he wholeheartedly condemned. He described how he had been made aware of the strike on the Saturday preceding the Thursday massacre. He had been told by Thibedi Ramontja, the Director General of the Department of Mineral Resources, that a 'terrible and distressing situation had developed at Marikana which had resulted in the violent deaths of two Lonmin security officers with attacks and disruptions continuing'.

There were fears that the killing of security officers and others would escalate because, without a greatly increased police presence, the violence could not be contained. Ramaphosa had been told by Ramontja that 'at this stage it is clear that probably only a massive police and possibly army presence will stop us having a repeat of recent past experiences or nearby, we simply do not have the capability to protect life and limb and I urge you to please use your influence to bring this over to the necessary officials who have the resources at their disposal. We need help.'

Ramaphosa was horrified at the prospect of more killings while the police dragged their feet. He sent a text message to Nathi Mthethwa that afternoon. The minister phoned him back two hours later and they had a five-minute conversation: 'He testified that during that conversation he raised the concern that Mr [Albert] Jamieson [chief commercial officer of Lonmin] had raised, that people had died and were dying and that the situation was getting worse. He mentioned that Mr Jamieson had requested that the police presence be increased so as to prevent further loss of life. He informed the Minister that the situation he had been told about on the ground was "such that they need help, they need more police presence on the ground".'

Ramaphosa was adamant that he did not suggest what steps should be taken and that he had only communicated concern over the unfolding violence and the need for some action to be taken. Ramaphosa's view was borne out by Mthethwa, who testified: 'I spoke to . . . Mr Ramaphosa, who had called earlier, or had left a message and I then returned the call. He explained to me that the situation in Marikana is bad. I'm not quoting his exact words, but he says he's concerned because people are dying there, property is being damaged there and as far as he can see there are no police, or adequate police on the ground.'

After hearing of further violence, Ramaphosa spoke with Mthethwa once more. In that conversation, he 'stressed that they should immediately take steps to ensure that they protect life and property and bring those responsible for the terrible acts of violence and deaths to book.' Before the commission, Ramaphosa explained what he had meant: 'When I said that they should be brought to book, I had anticipated and expected that those who were responsible would be identified and they would be arrested which is what I expect the police to do normally in pursuing their tasks and duties. It occurred to me that where these incidents had occurred, one got the full details thereof, police presence was either absent or very minimal and that is why I felt these people were being attacked and being killed in the way they were.'

Mthethwa testified that Ramaphosa had told him that he did not think that what was unfolding was 'pure industrial action in the true sense of the word: It had criminality on it and violence.' In an email to Albert Jamieson on the eve of the shooting, Ramaphosa wrote that 'all government officials need to understand that we are essentially dealing with a criminal act. I have said as much to the Minister of Safety and Security.'

Ramaphosa's interest in the policing of the Marikana strike was communicated to the police: 'Lieutenant General Mbombo said that she received a telephone call from Minister Mthethwa on the evening of 12 August in which the Minister told her that he had received a report from Mr Ramaphosa, asking if he knew about what was happening at Marikana and stating, "this appears to be a problem, he should please look carefully at it".' She had later taken this to mean that the minister was being 'pressurised' by Ramaphosa.

On the Monday before the shooting, Ramaphosa received a further email telling him that the death toll had risen to four. He also spoke to the Mineral Resources minister, Susan Shabangu, and had summarised this conversation in an email to a Lonmin manager: 'I called her and told her that her silence and inaction about what is happening at Lonmin was bad for her and the Government. She said that she was going to issue a statement. She was going to be in Cape Town to attend a Joint Parliamentary Session and would be back in Johannesburg later today to attend to the Lonmin matter. I told her that I would also be in Cape Town and suggested that we should have a discussion and see what she needs to do.'

In his evidence, Ramaphosa elaborated: 'The discussions I had with Minister Shabangu, who was then the Minister of Mineral Resources, were that the situation at Lonmin was deteriorating, more and more people were getting killed and injured and that was a matter of great concern to me because I knew how this type of situation can just escalate into more and more violence and I was saying that we need to make sure that at a government level we sensitise people so that the Minister of Police can be of assistance and deploy more police who can protect life and property.'

On the day before the massacre, Lonmin's Jamieson emailed Ramaphosa, thanking him for his help but citing 'two areas of concern': 'We are grateful the police now have [about 800 members] on site. Our next challenge is sustaining this and ensuring they remain and take appropriate action so we can get people back to work. It would be good to have some independent confirmation the police have plans to sustain a presence for at least a week and numbers don't wane by the weekend. If you can talk to the Minister please could you influence these things with her and encourage her to make time to talk to Roger [Phillimore, chairman of Lonmin]?'

It was in reply to this email that Ramaphosa used the phrase 'concomitant action'. His reply read: 'I thank you for the consistent manner in which you are characterising the current difficulties we are going through. The terrible events that have unfolded cannot be described as a labour dispute. They are plainly dastardly criminal and must be characterised as such. In line with this characterization there needs to be concomitant action to address this situation. You are absolutely correct in insisting that the Minister and indeed all government officials need to understand that we are essentially dealing with a criminal act. I have said as much to the Minister of Safety and Security. I will stress that Minister Shabangu should have a discussion with Roger.'

He later sent another email, which read: 'I have just had a discussion with Susan Shabangu in Cape Town. She agrees that what we are going through is not a labour dispute but a criminal act. She will correct her characterisation of what we are experiencing. She is going into Cabinet and will brief the President as well and get the Minister of Police Nathi Mthethwa to act in a more pointed way. She will be in Johannesburg by 5pm and would be able to speak to Roger. Let us keep the pressure on them to act correctly.' The phrase 'in a more pointed way' was construed by Ramaphosa's opponents to be more evidence that he wanted the police to take violent action.

In his evidence to the commission, he explained the comment as follows: 'I meant that what we wanted to communicate to government [was] that we're dealing with people who are being killed and what we need to do is to prevent further deaths occurring, and acting in a pointed way would mean that those who are perpetrating those acts should be arrested so that that comes to a stop and does not carry on any further. That is acting in a pointed way.'

He went on: 'I did not have anything further in mind except that the police need to do their job and as I understand it their job is to have a presence where acts of criminality are taking place, to prevent further acts of criminality and to arrest those who they know have perpetrated such acts so that they do not carry on perpetrating those acts. That is the sum total of what I expect the police to do.'

The commission remarked of Ramaphosa's comments: 'During his cross-examination, the email he sent to Mr Jamieson at 12h18 on 15 August was cited as indicating that he had wrongly referred to the labour dispute as being "dastardly criminal", and had said it had to be characterised as such and had to be addressed by "concomitant action". It is clear that the "terrible events" to which Mr Ramaphosa referred were the serious criminal offences, including murders which arose from attempts to enforce the unprotected strike by violence and intimidation. These events arose in the context of a labour dispute which resulted in the strike. But Mr Ramaphosa's reference to the "terrible events that have unfolded" cannot reasonably be construed as a reference to the labour dispute or the strike. As the evidence leaders correctly submitted "the words plainly refer to the murders and other acts of violence which had taken place. Those were indeed criminal acts and they did indeed need to be addressed in that fashion."'

The commission said it was in full agreement with the submission by the evidence leaders, which read as follows: 'If one excludes for the moment the clash between the strikers and the members of the SAPS on 13 August, to which particular considerations apply, five of the deaths had been the result of murders committed during the course of the strike. It cannot be contended that this was not a serious criminal matter, or that it was improper or inappropriate to seek to persuade the government to see the matter in that light.'

The report went on to state: 'We submit that it cannot be fairly suggested that the call for "concomitant action" to be taken in respect of murders and violence, involves the exercise of inappropriate political influence, or an attempt to have the police brought in to break the strike. In Mr Ramaphosa's capacity as a director of Lonmin, he may well have had a legal obligation to take what steps he could to prevent the killing or injuring of Lonmin's employees, the damaging of its property, and the damaging of its business.'

Ramaphosa's communication with ministers was also deemed 'not inappropriate or inadmissible': 'We submit that it is self-evident why it was Mr Ramaphosa, and not another Lonmin director or a Lonmin executive, who made the call to the Minister of Police on Sunday 12 August, and who met Minister Shabangu on Wednesday 15 August. He was a senior office-bearer of the African National Congress, and he knew the Ministers and other key role-players in government. As a result, he had access to them and influence with them. Suggestions to the contrary, for example that he had no greater access or influence than ordinary members of the people, are plainly fanciful.'

While the commission found that Ramaphosa did not bear any responsibility for the violent action taken by police, it did find that '[i]t may well be that the directors, and perhaps particularly Mr Ramaphosa given his background, should have appreciated the need for urgent action to address the underlying labour dispute, and should have intervened actively to ensure that management took such action. While the matter had to be dealt with in part as a policing matter, that was not likely to be sufficient. It was also necessary to address the underlying labour dispute.'

It also found that '[i]f what Mr Ramaphosa did was attempt to persuade the Minister to ensure that there should be greater police presence on the ground so as to prevent further loss of life, there was no incompatibility in the interests which he had in the matter. The interests of Lonmin, the African National Congress, and the interests of those with whom he had personal relationships, were not incompatible: they all had an interest in putting an end to the killings which had taken place. The only people who had an interest in a continuation of the killings were those who were carrying them out.'

The report described these interests as a 'confluence or an overlapping of interests': 'Mr Ramaphosa was correct in saying that if someone is trying to help solve a situation, which would save lives or would advance the common purpose of everyone, it should not be seen as a conflict of interests.' Ramaphosa, it found, had no knowledge of the decision made on Wednesday 15 August to move to the tactical option: 'However, it is likely that the precipitate (and still unexplained) decision of 15 August, to move to the "tactical phase" the following day if the strikers did not lay down their arms and leave the koppie, was at least partly the consequence of the senior police officials feeling the need to act and be seen to act. The telephonic discussion which Mr Ramaphosa had with the Minister, and the discussions which the Minister then had with Mr Zokwana and with the National and Provincial Commissioners, are likely well have been a factor in that decision.'

Ramaphosa, therefore, 'had no reason to believe that the SAPS would launch the precipitate, ill planned and poorly commanded operations, which caused the deaths of 34 strikers on 16 August.

In fact . . . in his email sent at 00h47 on 15 August to Mr Philli-more he stated that he had spoken to Mr Zokwana, the President of NUM, who said that he and Mr Frans Baleni, the Secretary General of NUM, wanted to meet him and Mr James Motlatsi, a former NUM President, on Friday, 17 August, "to discuss what they should do as a union going forward". This indicates that he did not envisage any sudden operation such as in fact took place on 16 August. This is also demonstrated by Mr Jamieson's email sent at 09h43 to Mr Ramaphosa where he said that "it would be good to have some independent confirmation the police have plans to sustain a presence for at least a week and numbers don't wane by the weekend".'

The final paragraphs of the Ramaphosa chapter read: 'There is no basis for the Commission to find even on a *prima facie* basis that Mr Ramaphosa is guilty of the crimes he is alleged to have committed. The Commission agrees with the submissions by Mr Ramaphosa's counsel that the accusations made against him by counsel for the Injured and Arrested persons are groundless.' It was a resounding declaration of Ramaphosa's innocence by a commission whose credibility was accepted by most, but the months of harsh criticism had cut deep.

\*

Years later, Ramaphosa still bore the scars from those cuts and continued to suffer their ill effects. The criticism framed him as a capitalist insider who had thrown out his principles and now wore the cloak of the oppressor he had once fought as the champion of mineworkers. So deep were the wounds that, in May 2017, when he began to campaign seriously for the ANC presidency, Rama-phosa felt the need to offer a full apology to the victims of Mari-kana, after being urged to do so by Winnie Madikizela-Mandela and the NUM.

Interviewed by Bongani Madondo for the *Sunday Times* in June 2017, Ramaphosa was asked about the Marikana 'monkey on your back'. He replied: 'There's just no limit to that apology. What happened is indescribable. It was terrible. It will remain a black dot in our narrative. I take full responsibility of my role in it, and once again, my role was as follows. I was disturbed upon hearing the news that ten miners, ten innocent miners, had been killed. My reaction was: this cannot be activism. This is a criminal act. Back then I felt that the situation should be dealt with by the law. It was inappropriate language. I cannot try to be smart about it.'[4]

Madondo didn't leave it there, saying: 'Talk me through your apology.'

Ramaphosa replied: 'Although I had apologised before and took full responsibility, two major guides I have much respect and love for approached me. It was Mama Winnie Mandela and, separately, the National Union of Mineworkers who came to me and said: "Hey, Ndoda, you have to address this with the nation." And I immediately said: "Yes, Mama." I had already heard the NUM out and agreed with them. So, the stars aligned, the heart still sank deeper knowing human life, for whatever reason and under whatever circumstances it was taken, cannot be brought back. I'm still apologetic even now. I also believe there are several people, including me and entities that, in the process of initiating healing and hearing out families still traumatised, have started individual means of moving ahead, mostly subject to the families' subjective response to this. If it was bad for me, imagine how terrible it is for them.'

On the subject of his emails and his use of the phrase 'concomitant action', Ramaphosa said: 'I meant that we are losing [the] grip of law and order in the area. Since ten people were already killed, I feared for a worse bloodbath. It was an interventionist impulse. Some people say I was protecting Shanduka's investment in Lonmin. Of course, that's being nasty and creative with the facts. Truth be said, we lost money, R300 million of what was invested was subsequently underwritten. We are not complaining. Money cannot be equal to, nor be a substitute to, human or any other life. But it cannot be said that we were protecting profits; what profits?'

Joseph Mathunjwa, president of Amcu, which was behind the Marikana strike, rejected Ramaphosa's apology: 'As an African, Ramaphosa knows he should have started by seeking the forgiveness of families of miners.'[5]

*

Marikana was the low point of Ramaphosa's political life. It became a stick that political enemies would beat him with. The claim that Ramaphosa actively sought the shooting of the mineworkers was clearly untrue. The exhaustive exploration of this subject by the Farlam Commission proved this comprehensively. Perhaps Ramaphosa was guilty of something else – of taking his eye off the ball. Any diligent director – especially one who had founded the country's first mineworkers' union – ought to have seen the crisis building and acted a lot sooner to defuse it. Ramaphosa's real failing was that he was, in the words of Michael Spicer, 'an absentee landlord'.

In 2016, the veteran journalist Greg Marinovich published the most comprehensive account of the Marikana shooting in the book *Murder at Small Koppie*. It would go on win the country's leading prize for non-fiction, the Alan Paton Award. Ramaphosa had said he was surprised to discover 'the huge differential between the wages paid to the rock drill operators in other companies and what we pay them', as he wrote in an email to a Lonmin representative on the company's executive management committee. Marinovich observed: 'But he should have known. As chair of the transformation committee from 2010, he was meant to hold management accountable for the social conditions of workers and the communities around the mine.'[6] He concluded: 'Ramaphosa should have insisted, at the very least Lonmin speak to their striking employees. He did not. Ramaphosa, it would seem, acted to protect his own financial interests, to protect NUM from the workers' ire, and to enable the ANC's legislated patronage to continue unhindered.'[7]

The Marikana crisis exposed Ramaphosa to unprecedented criticism. Perhaps the Ramaphosa of old, the man who had left politics for business after failing to win the deputy presidency back in 1994, might have turned his back on this episode and gone into his shell. But he was now too close to achieving the goal of becoming president, which he had shelved after he was sidelined by Mbeki all those years ago. All he had to do was to play his cards right with Jacob Zuma and hope that the stain of the latter's reputation would not contaminate him. He was heading back to politics to claim the prize that had been rudely taken from his hands 20 years earlier. This time, he would play to win.

SEVEN
# *Return to politics*

And people in branches stood up and discussed the pros and the
cons of having a Cyril Ramaphosa standing as deputy president.
When that happened and there was just a flood, a flood of
support, I got the sense that this is the voice that I needed to
heed. – *Cyril Ramaphosa*

When the news broke, it beggared belief. Thabo Mbeki's presidency
was, on the face of it a great success. He presided over the longest
sustained period of economic growth, witnessed more people than
ever before enter the labour market, initiated the African Renais-
sance and brought structure to the post-Mandela government. But,
instead of thriving on these successes, Mbeki began to show signs
of paranoia. He did not believe that 'Western' scientists had proved
that the HIV virus caused Aids and he fought tooth and nail against
efforts to extend treatment to those who were vulnerable. And, in
2001, he associated himself with the view that there was a plot to
oust him from the presidency, led by Cyril Ramaphosa and two
other ANC heavyweights, Tokyo Sexwale and Mathews Phosa.

The world was beginning to recalibrate its view of South Africa
as the miracle nation that had grown up in the shadow of Nelson
Mandela. This is how London's *Guardian* newspaper reported news
of the 'coup plot': 'The South African government has ordered the
investigation of three leading anti-apartheid politicians, including
the former secretary general of the African National Congress Cyril
Ramaphosa, who is now a monitor of the IRA's weapons dumps,[1]

for allegedly plotting to physically harm and oust President Thabo Mbeki. The investigation was immediately denounced as an attempt to use the police to suppress legitimate political challenges to Mr Mbeki's leadership of the ANC.'[2]

For Ramaphosa, the news came as bombshell: 'Oh, my lord! It was bizarre. It was a complete bolt from the blue. I was in Cape Town when it happened, but I did not even realise that something was brewing and building up.'[3] Ramaphosa, Phosa and Sexwale were all in business by this time, having one by one fallen out with the increasingly erratic Mbeki. Unsurprisingly, they bumped into each other and they talked. But a return to politics was the furthest thing from Ramaphosa's mind. Now in the seventh year of his business career, he was about to launch his big conglomerate, Shanduka.

Ramaphosa immediately went to see Mandela: 'I said: "What do you make of this?" And he said: "Keep calm", because I'd wanted to respond, issue a statement. He said: "Do not issue a statement. Keep calm. Let me deal with this."' Ramaphosa backed down from action while Mandela sought to get to the bottom of the problem.

He took stock. 'It shocked me. It actually shocked me to my very core that people thought that I would want to undo precisely what we had painstakingly built as a movement to put in place – a new government that would transform this country. For me it was scary. Not only unsettling, but scary. It was scary because I started having visions of being arrested, being put before a court for treason and I thought: "This is when the revolution eats its own children."'

He approached Kgalema Motlanthe, his old comrade from the NUM, who was now secretary general of the ANC, and tried to meet with Mbeki, but hit a brick wall. Mbeki, meanwhile, in a national television interview, confirmed that an investigation was under way. In the end, the probe was withdrawn and Mbeki's stature was diminished just as his economic programme began to bear fruit. It was all a senseless waste of political capital.

129

The 'coup plot' was a bracing reminder to Ramaphosa of why he had walked away from the leadership politics within the ANC. But, once Mbeki left the political stage, to be replaced by Jacob Zuma, the dynamic changed. Within the ANC, there was growing criticism of Zuma as scandal after scandal hit the headlines. The ANC, once seemingly invincible at the polls, was beginning to lose electoral support for the first time.

*

In December 2012, Cyril Ramaphosa made a dramatic return to the political stage and was elected ANC deputy president at the party's congress in Mangaung. The prodigal son's journey had been some months in the making.

After Jacob Zuma defeated Thabo Mbeki for the ANC presidency at Polokwane in September 2007, Zuma took the decision to recall Mbeki as president of the country the following year. Zuma did not immediately assume the presidency, opting to give the job to Kgalema Motlanthe until the 2009 general election. Motlanthe proved a loyal lieutenant, and it was on his watch that key Zuma policies were implemented. It was Motlanthe, for example, who signed off on legislation disbanding the Scorpions, the independent corruption-fighting unit that had investigated the corruption charges against Zuma. The unit was replaced by the Hawks, which reported directly to the police and did not work in the 'FBI style' of the Scorpions, which had operational independence and which had worked directly with national prosecutors. It was also on Motlanthe's watch that the acting head of the National Prosecuting Authority (NPA), Mokotedi Mpshe, announced the dropping of all corruption charges against Zuma, clearing the way for him to take over from Motlanthe after the 2009 general election.

Ramaphosa's return to national political prominence occurred in April 2012 when he chaired an ANC disciplinary appeals committee. The hearing was to decide the fate of then ANC Youth League leader, Julius Malema, and others, who had been found guilty of causing divisions in the party the previous November. Malema, once a fervent Zuma supporter who vowed to kill and die for him, had fallen out with the president, whom he now frequently publicly criticised. Malema had gone so far as to compare Zuma unfavourably with his predecessor, Thabo Mbeki.

Malema's appeal backfired when the appeals committee led by Ramaphosa chose to turn the original five-year suspension into expulsion from the party. In announcing the committee's decision, which was televised live, Ramaphosa said: 'The NDCA [National Disciplinary Committee of Appeal] is of the view that it was reasonable to have regard to Malema's recurring pattern of similar conduct since November 10 last year. The immediate suspension would put a stop to the recurring pattern of Malema's behaviour and obviate any further damage to the good name and reputation of the ANC. When Malema joined the ANC, he subjected himself to the ANC constitution and its code of conduct; in doing so, he voluntarily agreed to limit his freedom of expression apropos his relationship with the ANC.'[4]

Ramaphosa appeared to be holding the party line on discipline. By getting rid of Malema, he no doubt pleased the political establishment, which did not want to see the rabble-rousing populist youth becoming a contender for an ANC leadership position and – as Zuma himself had once predicted – a future leader of the party.

But Ramaphosa had also done Zuma a big favour. With nine months to go before the Mangaung conference, Malema could have become a focal point for mobilisation against Zuma's presidency. He had been the highly effective fulcrum of the campaign to elect Zuma, and the spectre of Malema doing this for a rival must have caused nervousness.

This rival would turn out to be Kgalema Motlanthe, who had

fallen out with Zuma, apparently over the latter's failure to address growing criticism of his personal gain from the refurbishment of his Nkandla homestead in KwaZulu-Natal, and over other matters such as the push for legislation to clamp down on media freedom in the name of state security. Motlanthe also disagreed with the expulsion of Malema. Fairly late in 2012, and after months of prevarication, Motlanthe threw his hat in the ring. He would stand against Zuma for the party presidency.

As the conference approached, it became clear that Motlanthe would not strike a deal to stay out of the race. Zuma and his supporters began to cast around for a candidate they could place on their slate who would demonstrate ethnic inclusivity and counter the popular appeal of Motlanthe. Although softly spoken, Motlanthe had a strong following among the party's committed activists because of his ability to convey complicated intellectual concepts in struggle language. He was seen as a deep thinker who was not personally ambitious so much as pursuing the rebirth and purification of the party.

To counter Motlanthe, the Zuma camp hit on Ramaphosa, by now a successful businessman, who shared a similar early political profile to Motlanthe; both had been general secretaries of the NUM. The word was that it was the ANC's powerful provincial chairman in KwaZulu-Natal, Zweli Mkhize, who persuaded Ramaphosa to join the ticket and run for the deputy presidency.[5] Ramaphosa took the bait.

Ramaphosa's decision to expel Malema from the party might have earned him Zuma's trust, but it would come back to haunt him later that year following the Marikana massacre. Malema would lead the charge against Ramaphosa, accusing him of ordering the killings in emails calling for 'concomitant action'. Malema's caricature of the rich, powerful and aloof Ramaphosa cynically protecting his wealth struck a popular chord.

Malema was a canny operator. Not only was he getting his revenge on the man who had expelled him from the party, but he was also laying the groundwork for the post-Zuma era. Ramaphosa would likely be the next president of the country and some way needed to be found to make him a target of public antipathy.

The Zuma camp's Ramaphosa strategy was spectacularly on the money. Zuma defeated Motlanthe by 2 978 votes to 900, while Ramaphosa defeated his two rivals for the deputy presidency, Tokyo Sexwale and Mathews Phosa. What was astonishing – and perhaps a little alarming for Zuma – was that Ramaphosa received 3 018 votes – 40 more than he did.[6]

*

When I spoke to Ramaphosa between his election as ANC deputy president and the start of his term as deputy president of the country, he said he had not planned to come back to full-time politics: 'I resisted it for quite some time. When some of the power brokers in the ANC started peddling my name around, I still resisted and for some reason I kept hoping that for some reason, Kgalema Motlanthe would not stand against Zuma and he would go back and be deputy president.'

He said he changed his mind when he realised there was grass-roots support for him. He began to think again 'when the branches of the ANC started their nomination processes, the 4 500 branches, as they started their nomination processes, and my name started coming up more and more and I started getting reports that I was actually being thoroughly discussed in the various branches.' He continued: 'And people in branches stood up and discussed the pros and the cons of having a Cyril Ramaphosa standing as deputy president. When that happened and there was just a flood, a flood of support, I got the sense that this is the voice that I needed to heed. And people were basically saying: "You've been in business, you've done well in business, you have achieved good things in business, we want you now to come and serve the nation more broadly."'

Ramaphosa said he 'heeded that call' and that his motivation was 'not even really being driven by the quest for power, or whatever, it's just been: go back and serve the people. Which is what drove me to become secretary general of the NUM. I could have gone off and led a very simple and pleasant life as a lawyer, defended whatever case and made a lot of money as a lawyer, but I decided that I'd like to go and serve mineworkers. The same thing has motivated me.'

Ramaphosa was aware that, for the ANC, he represented the hope that its dwindling support among middle-class South Africans might be bolstered: 'I'm hoping that my own participation and the message I will be spreading around will be convincing enough to that cohort of the middle class that might feel disgruntled and feel that, you know, they need to put their support elsewhere. If they look at the record, even the landed white middle class since 1994 has not done badly. In fact, they have thrived. So, this is a party that allows even a middle class to thrive.'

The ANC was beginning to develop the line that there was 'a good story to tell' about South Africa since 1994 and Ramaphosa echoed that: 'Have we done it successfully in the last twenty years? I believe we have. The fact that so many people have been lifted out of poverty into the middle class and that even those who are still very poor are able to get by through the efforts of the government, of the ruling party in the form of grants, in the form of facilities, services. Although some of those services are not being delivered as effectively as the party itself would want them to be delivered. And that is a problem we need to address. We can address it and we can make things better.'

Ramaphosa's take on service delivery protests, which suggested that the party narrative was not entirely justified, seemed to stretch the political elastic a little too far: 'No good deed goes unpunished. You go to some of these areas. I mean they've got roads and all of that and we say: "Why are you protesting?" And they say: "We want more." And they deserve more. I support them, they deserve more. It's like when you've become used to the good life you want everything that's better. There's nothing wrong with that.'

\*

The real issue that Ramaphosa would have to confront was, without question, the growing crisis of corruption. Back in 2013, fresh into his deputy presidency, he was still toeing the party line. The ANC had, by then, ceased to deny that it was mired in corruption. The new narrative was that the party was painfully aware of the growing corruption problem and was determined to do all it could to root it out. Ramaphosa observed: 'The situation that we are operating in – the environment and the circumstances – have changed and the ANC has had, over the years, to acclimatise itself to a changed situation. We are now a ruling party. We're no longer a party on the outside and the sins of incumbency begin to seep in. There's complacency. The sins of incumbency then accumulate. We're being slow in dealing with slack performance, incompetence and corruption as a ruling party.'

The ANC's new position, that it was open and transparent about corruption, was a fallback that allowed the party to play the victim, as if it had merely been naive and some external agency had taken it off-guard. Ramaphosa again: 'The good thing in all of that is that the ANC itself has recognised some of these ills. It has done a thorough analysis and in many ways, has done it so transparently, so openly. Not many parties that I know of would be able to say: "We've become victims of the sins of incumbency, we've become lax when it comes to our competence and performance."'

He was, however, already beginning to put some distance between himself and the party, if you were prepared to read through the royal 'we': 'We've been a bit tolerant in certain cases of corrupt acts. There's been indiscipline in the party and there have been divisions in the party, there's been factionalism in the party and all that.' At that point, soon after Ramaphosa became ANC deputy president, unhappiness with Zuma was growing but had not yet reached a crescendo and Ramaphosa was arguing for an integrity commission and for greater discipline within the party. The commission would eventually be established and would call for tough action against Zuma, but would be rendered toothless by the unwillingness of the party's top leadership to empower it.

Back then, in 2013, Ramaphosa was still speaking the language of ANC spin when it came to ethics: 'We call this decade, the decade of the cadre. What does it mean? It means that we long to go back to the high moral standards, high values of the founding fathers – and mothers – of the ANC. We will get there and we are on the way to rebuilding those values and those ethics. We will move quicker and get the *Titanic* to move around. We will get there.'

Ramaphosa's game plan appeared to be to stay strictly inside the party's running lanes, building himself up as an insider. He needed to win Zuma's trust if he was to be made his deputy in government – something that was not a certainty, although it had become an informal tradition. For those who were hoping that Ramaphosa would return to the ANC as a new broom, sweeping the party clean with a barnstorming assault on its corrupt establishment, years of disappointment lay ahead.

*

After the 2014 general election, it became clear that Zuma would follow tradition and appoint Ramaphosa deputy president of the country. Lindiwe Zulu, then a trusted Zuma adviser and later a

Cabinet minister, made it clear that 'Cyril is likely to be the deputy president in line with ANC procedure, because whoever has been elected the president or deputy president in the party takes up that position in government. There hasn't been any indication that he will not take up the position. President Zuma and the country needs a strong deputy in cabinet.'[7] In an unusually candid statement for an ANC insider, Zulu openly admitted that Ramaphosa would help the party win back lost votes: 'The ANC is shaken up by the loss in support and we are doing analysis on how we can improve and do better for our people. Cyril's leadership could help the ANC get back the support it lost in these past elections. There is definitely room for the ANC to make a comeback especially in provinces like Gauteng.'[8]

There were already alarming signs that the ANC was losing ground in the country's economic heartland. In Gauteng, the party's support had shrunk from 64 per cent to 53 per cent of the vote. The possibility of this slipping below 50 per cent, thereby allowing an opposition coalition to take control of Johannesburg or Tshwane, was alarming for the ruling party.

On 25 May 2014, Ramaphosa was sworn in as deputy president. He would become the leader of government business in the National Assembly and was placed in charge of the National Planning Commission, which produced the much-praised National Development Plan. Not long afterwards, Ramaphosa would once again clash with Julius Malema, this time over the national anthem.

During the negotiations over South Africa's transition from apartheid to democracy, a new national anthem had been developed, combining 'Nkosi Sikelel' iAfrika' (God Bless Africa), which the ANC had adopted, with the national anthem of the apartheid state, 'Die Stem van Suid-Afrika' (The Call of South Africa). Malema called for the Afrikaans portion of the anthem to be scrapped.

137

The lyrics of this section were politically inoffensive. Translated into English, they read: 'Out of the blue of our heavens, Out of the depths of our seas, Over everlasting mountains, Where the echoing crags resound.' Malema's objection appeared to be that this portion of the anthem carried an association with the apartheid state. Ramaphosa countered with: 'We are about building a nation and we must extend a hand of friendship, a hand of continued reconciliation to those who feel that the national anthem does not represent them any longer, and it can happen on both sides.' Ramaphosa's feud with Malema was rumbling on.

\*

Ramaphosa's calculation appears to have been that obtaining the deputy presidency of the party – even if this meant serving Zuma and risking the accompanying political contamination – would provide him with the best launching pad for the presidency when Zuma's term ended in 2017 (his term as president of the country was due to run until 2019). But it would be a treacherous, rocky road. According to this 'insider' strategy, Ramaphosa would have to suck it up and stand behind Zuma, never directing criticism at him personally. He would have to confine himself to abstract comments about the Constitution being paramount and the rule of law needing to be applied.

While he played this 'inside' game, many who might otherwise have supported him would come out and openly criticise Zuma and the Guptas, risking their positions and opening themselves up to politically motivated criminal investigations and intelligence dirty tricks. Ramaphosa's 'inside' game would eventually have to give way to open criticism. The ANC was entering a crisis the likes of which it had never seen before.

# EIGHT
## *Crisis point*

Our people are watching in fear, wondering if we are still capable
of leading them. They hear in our language, in our ideas, a
hankering after past victories and past glory – yet they long most
of all to hear about the future. – *Cyril Ramaphosa*

There is an old photograph of a group of men and women arranged
in front of a South African flag. They appear to be in high spirits.
Seated in the front row is a much younger Cyril Ramaphosa. Seated
in the middle is Pravin Gordhan. Also in the picture are Joe Slovo,
Mac Maharaj, Fanie van der Merwe and Roelf Meyer. The photograph is of the management team of the Transitional Executive
Council, and was taken on the occasion of choosing South Africa's
new flag on the eve of the first democratic election.

Ramaphosa, widely credited as the leading architect of the Constitution, and Gordhan, then an immensely effective organiser on
behalf of the ANC, had reason to look pleased with themselves.
They had steered the negotiations to a conclusion, and South
Africa was about to become a constitutional state where democracy and human rights were entrenched and each person had an
equal vote in elections. This was not a foregone conclusion when
a profusion of homeland, white establishment and liberation parties began talks over South Africa's future.

Fast forward twenty-four years. Two of the men who appear in
the photograph are part of a complex political entanglement at

the centre of which stands the Constitution they brought into being. South Africa has become a constitutional state, with the Constitutional Court at the apex of the judiciary and therefore the country's final arbiter on matters pertaining to its social and political development when these collide with the law.

Cyril Ramaphosa's journey has taken several unexpected turns. After the finalisation of the Constitution by the new democratic Parliament in 1996, he left the political stage to embark on a business career during which he built an empowerment empire before returning to politics at the ANC's 2012 conference. He found himself in a highly charged political environment. By this time, the Zuma controversy had gripped the country for more than seven years. It had erupted in 2005, when Jacob Zuma was fired as deputy president of the country by Thabo Mbeki following the conviction of Zuma's financial adviser, Schabir Shaik, on three charges of corruption. The person whom Schaik was found to have corrupted was Zuma, who was expected to create favourable circumstances for Shaik's company to benefit from the massive arms deal of 1999. But Zuma somehow escaped being charged, despite the 783 counts of corruption that the corruption-busting Scorpions had compiled.

Zuma, who had failed to matriculate at school, had been stereotyped as a rural simpleton who blundered his way about politics. This proved to be a serious underestimation of his political nous. Zuma had done time on Robben Island where he had, in common with many of his fellow political prisoners, read and studied hard. He had become an excellent chess player. On his release, he had headed the exiled ANC's intelligence department where he was privy to the dalliances of his fellow exiles. On his return to the country, he had played a central role in defusing political violence between the ANC and Inkatha in KwaZulu-Natal, which had claimed hundreds of lives prior to the transition.

In one of the greatest political comebacks of modern times, Zuma went from being dismissed and disgraced to wrenching the presidency away from Mbeki after a political campaign that blended populism, opportunism and even ethnicity into a cocktail that most ANC delegates at its 2007 conference gleefully imbibed. Not only did Zuma have to overcome the ignominy of being dismissed, but he also had his name dragged through the mud in a rape trial during which it was found he had sex with a young family friend without using protection despite knowing that she carried the HIV virus. Zuma mounted a highly successful campaign to project himself as the victim of political manipulation by Mbeki, who was accused of perverting the criminal justice system into fighting his political battles.

The battle between Mbeki and Zuma came to a head at the ANC's Polokwane conference in 2007, when the party elected a new leadership. Mbeki had indicated his intention to seek a third term as party president, and the run-up to the conference had been marked by ugly smears and political dirty tricks. The conference had about it the air of a beer-hall putsch, as delegates shouted down pro-Mbeki speakers and chanted divisive slogans while Zuma sang an old struggle song about a machine gun.

Mbeki was stunned when most delegates – by a handsome majority – voted in favour of Zuma. Few observers were surprised, though. Mbeki had made himself unpopular by alienating one constituency after another within the party as he sought to sideline potential competitors. Mbeki had been the architect of his own political isolation, first with his bizarre allegations against Ramaphosa and others that they were plotting to unseat him, and later when the left rejected his economic agenda. Zuma had assembled these rejected souls into what some described as 'a coalition of the wounded'.

For a time, Mbeki carried on as head of state, while Zuma was ensconced as party leader in Luthuli House, in downtown Johannesburg. Zuma then compounded Mbeki's humiliation by terminating his presidency in September 2008, after a judge ruled that Zuma had been the victim of Mbeki's manipulation of the Scorpions anti-corruption unit. This judgment was to be overturned in the strongest language by the Supreme Court of Appeal, but by then Mbeki was gone and Kgalema Motlanthe – himself a member of the 'coalition of the wounded' – had been installed as a caretaker president.

Zuma, through Motlanthe, set about dismantling the independence of the country's law enforcement agencies, overseeing the disbanding of the Scorpions. His usefulness at an end, Motlanthe handed the presidency over to Zuma after the 2009 general election. Zuma continued his efforts to weaken the criminal justice capacity of the state – especially that part of it which might want to reinstate the corruption charges against him – by appointing a succession of weak leaders to head the NPA.

The 'coalition of the wounded' included the SACP's Blade Nzimande and the head of Cosatu, Zwelinzima Vavi. Both had bought into the idea that Zuma promised a new left direction for the state, which they believed Mbeki had suborned to the will of the country's business elite. Their ire was particularly directed at the Gear policy – dubbed the '1996 class project' – which was seen by the left as conceding too much control over economic policy to international financial markets. Their eyes were soon to be opened, however, as Zuma failed to carve out a clear economic direction, choosing instead to busy himself by generating one scandal after another.

By the time Ramaphosa entered the Cabinet, Zuma was engulfed in controversy over the spending of some R250 million of public money on the renovation and expansion of his homestead at Nkandla in KwaZulu-Natal. It was a scandal that soon became a full-blown crisis.

*

The state undertook renovations on Zuma's Nkandla residence, ostensibly to improve its security. The contractors did very little to make the place safer, although it could be argued that police housing, roads and security fencing were legitimate parts of the construction plan. Instead they built a large swimming pool, an amphitheatre, a cattle kraal and an enclosure for chickens, among other extras. It was a project where the contractors appeared to operate without oversight, substantially overcharging for their work under the lax supervision of the state, which appeared to be humouring Zuma's desire to build a rural idyll where he might one day retire. The bills began to spiral out of control and soon become the subject of press reports. Nkandla, once the name of a rural village, would become a byword for corruption under Zuma.

In December 2009, the *Mail & Guardian* broke the news of the overspending, under the headline 'Zuma's R65 million Nkandla Splurge'.[1] As the scandal widened, so the numbers grew. By the time the matter was investigated by the Public Protector, spending was north of R250 million.

Zuma had appointed Advocate Thuli Madonsela, a former ANC MP, to the position of Public Protector in 2009, but she had – unlike her lackadaisical predecessor, Lawrence Mushwana – begun to demonstrate a courageous and fearless independence. When complaints about the spending on Nkandla reached her office, she undertook an investigation. In March 2014, in a nationally televised broadcast, she issued a report under the title 'Secure in Comfort'. Zuma and his ministers had attempted to delay the report or to undermine it by initiating other investigations conducted by lackeys, and by attacking the position of the Public

Protector. One notorious intervention even claimed Madonsela was a CIA agent. The Deputy Minister of Defence and Military Veterans, Kebby Maphatsoe, said: 'We can't allow people to hijack the ANC. We'll fight and defend the African National Congress. *uThuli umele asitshele ukuthi ubani ihandler yakhe* [Thuli must tell us who her handler is].'[2]

It was a defining moment for post-apartheid South Africa.

The Public Protector is a 'Chapter Nine' institution, the name coming from Chapter Nine of the Constitution, which empowers it to act independently and which makes its rulings carry substantial legal weight. In her report on Nkandla, Madonsela found: 'It is difficult not to reach the conclusion that a license to loot situation was created by government due to a lack of demand management by the organs of state involved.'[3]

She went on to detail how many of the facilities constructed could not be regarded as security features. It was a scouring report, which painstakingly pursued every line of questioning on how decisions were made in the government command chain, finding them lacking. She found that the renovations had not been legally compliant, that those involved in the project had 'failed dismally' to follow government's own supply chain management rules, that many buildings went 'beyond what is reasonably required for security' and that the expenditure was 'unconscionable, excessive and caused a misappropriation of public funds'.[4] The report continued: 'The allegation that the excessive expenditure added substantial value to the President's private property at the expense of the state is substantiated.'[5]

The ministers of Police and Public Works, as well as several high-ranking members of their departments, had failed to play their oversight role. Then came the bombshell: 'It is my considered view that as the President tacitly accepted the implementation of all measures at his residence and has unduly benefited from the enormous capital investment from the non-security installations at his private residence, a reasonable part of the expenditure towards the installations that were not identified as security measures in the list compiled by security experts in pursuit of the security evaluation, should be borne by him and his family.'[6]

The recommendation that Zuma should have to pay for part of the construction caused a national sensation. She ordered that he must 'take steps, with the assistance of the National Treasury and the SAPS, to determine the reasonable cost of the measures implemented by the Department of Public Works at his Nkandla residence that do not relate to security, and which include the Visitors Centre, the amphitheatre, the cattle kraal, the chicken run and the swimming pool'.[7]

Public demands for Zuma to 'pay back the money' grew louder, and would eventually be expressed in loud, unruly disruptions of Parliament by the opposition. But Zuma did nothing of the sort. Instead he asked his Police minister, Nkosinathi Nhleko, to conduct his own investigation into the Nkandla report. What followed was high farce. The minister reported that all the features were indeed security measures. A video was released showing firemen pumping water from the swimming pool, to the strains of 'O Sole Mio', ostensibly to prove that the installation was in fact a 'fire pool' that was built to deal with an emergency.

The ANC's majority in Parliament ensured that Madonsela's report was not adopted. Instead, lawmakers chose to go with the Cabinet cover-up. The opposition took the matter to the Constitutional Court, leading to one of the greatest court dramas of modern South Africa. The core matter to be decided was whether or not the remedial action ordered by the Public Protector was binding on Zuma.

*

On 13 March 2016, the nation came to a standstill to watch the Chief Justice, Mogoeng Mogoeng, deliver his judgment. His would be one of the most concise, forceful and elegant rulings to come from a South African bench: 'Constitutionalism, accountability and the rule of law constitute the sharp and mighty sword that stands ready to chop the ugly head of impunity off its stiffened neck,'[8] he told a rapt courtroom.

The judgment turned to the role of the president of the republic: 'The President is the Head of State and Head of the national Executive. His is indeed the highest calling to the highest office in the land. He is the first citizen of this country and occupies a position indispensable for the effective governance of our democratic country. Only upon him has the constitutional obligation to uphold, defend and respect the Constitution as the supreme law of the Republic been expressly imposed. The promotion of national unity and reconciliation falls squarely on his shoulders. As does the maintenance of orderliness, peace, stability and devotion to the well-being of the Republic and all its people. Unsurprisingly, the nation pins its hopes on him to steer the country in the right direction and accelerate our journey towards a peaceful, just and prosperous destination, that all other progress-driven nations strive towards on a daily basis. He is a constitutional being by design, a national pathfinder, the quintessential commander-in-chief of State affairs and the personification of this nation's constitutional project.'[9]

Of the Public Protector, Mogoeng said: 'She is the embodiment of a biblical David, that the public is, who fights the most powerful and very well-resourced Goliath, that impropriety and corruption by government officials are. The Public Protector is one of the true crusaders and champions of anticorruption and clean governance.'[10]

The National Assembly was not spared: 'On a proper construction of its constitutional obligations, the National Assembly was duty-bound to hold the President accountable by facilitating and ensuring compliance with the decision of the Public Protector.'[11]

Mogoeng ruled that 'The remedial action taken by the Public Protector against President Jacob Gedleyihlekisa Zuma in terms of section 182(1)(c) of the Constitution is binding.' Zuma's failure to comply with Madonsela's recommended remedial action was 'inconsistent with section 83(b) of the Constitution read with sections 181(3) and 182(1)(c) of the Constitution and is invalid.'[12] He ordered that the National Treasury was to determine the 'reasonable costs' of the measures not related to security, 'namely the visitors' centre, the amphitheatre, the cattle kraal, the chicken run and the swimming pool' and that Zuma was to pay this money back.[13]

When Ramaphosa and his fellow negotiators had drafted the Constitution some 20 years previously, they probably never envisaged a president being hauled over the coals in this manner. It was a tribute to their far-sightedness that they had stiffened the Constitution's spine against the abuse of executive power. But now that the Constitution had been used to curb Zuma's excesses, Ramaphosa was strangely quiet – in public at least. The word was that he had aired his unhappiness behind the scenes within the ANC's top structures, but that was where it had stopped.

It was not uncommon to hear from insiders that Ramaphosa and Zuma weren't talking, that they 'hated each other'. But, in public, Ramaphosa was silent. If his body language was considered, he appeared supportive – sharing a laugh, leaning over to confide in Zuma, being the model ANC citizen. The trouble was that fewer and fewer of Zuma's critics were prepared to play the game of false politics. After the judgment, many of them openly broke ranks. Led by the likes of Cheryl Carolus and Derek Hanekom, they began to publicly state their disapproval of Zuma's behaviour. The effect of this was to place Ramaphosa's manufactured bonhomie in stark relief.

*

Concern about Zuma's abuses had been building up for some time prior to the March 2016 Constitutional Court judgment. As the controversy swirled, senior ANC leaders began to speak out.

Zuma's choice of Ramaphosa as his deputy had been supposed to stave off controversy by suggesting that the country's future would be in the safe hands of Ramaphosa. At that point, it was the view of the party that the deputy president was the person anointed to succeed the president.

The other man at the centre of the growing crisis was Pravin Gordhan. After an exemplary tenure as Commissioner of the South African Revenue Service (SARS) from 1999 to 2009, he served as Finance minister during Zuma's first term as president. After the 2014 general election, he was moved to the Cooperative Governance and Traditional Affairs portfolio, while Nhlanhla Nene took up the reins at Finance. On 9 December 2015, Zuma made a grave error of judgement: he fired Nhlanhla Nene and replaced him with an unknown backbencher, David (Des) van Rooyen. The resulting crisis, dubbed 'Nenegate', saw the value of the rand plunge and billions wiped off the value of investments. After three days of market turmoil and opposition within his own party, Ramaphosa and ANC treasurer Zweli Mkhize essentially read Zuma the riot act; they had been approached by business leaders to intervene because of the dire consequences the decision held for the rand and South Africa's credit rating. Zuma relented and reappointed Gordhan as Finance minister on 14 December 2015.

Gordhan set about repairing the damage caused by Zuma's ill-advised assault on the National Treasury. On being appointed, Gordhan said: 'The facts about the developments that took place last week and the response of the financial markets are well known. Our currency fell, the stock market dropped by 2.94 per cent and bond yields shot up by over 150 basis points. We will stay the course of sound fiscal management. Our expenditure ceiling is sacrosanct.'[14]

A month later, Gordhan was asked whether market volatility was the result of Zuma's actions. He replied: 'The rand does not operate on what an individual does or says . . . but there are a wider set of factors that are at play.'[15] It was a diplomatic answer typical of Gordhan, who went out of his way to appear willing to work with Zuma.

Despite Gordhan's approach, it soon became apparent that Zuma regretted being forced to change his Cabinet decision. His original plan had been to place the pliable Van Rooyen in the Treasury to break down its tradition of independence from political influence. This was in line with Zuma's systematic placement of loyalists in charge of public enterprises. A prime example was the appointment of Dudu Myeni – the head of the Friends of Jacob Zuma Trust – to head South African Airways (SAA). Myeni's tenure was unimpressive, and the airline lurched from one financial crisis to another. She attempted to renege on a contract for the purchase of new planes by inserting a 'middle man' of uncertain financial pedigree into the transaction. The Treasury refused to sign off on this dodgy transaction. This and several other shows of independence by the Treasury, such as its continuing scrutiny of power utility Eskom, had irked Zuma. Van Rooyen was supposed to end this stand-off in Zuma's favour, in order, critics said, to open the spending taps for the benefit of Zuma and his cronies.

But, instead of Van Rooyen, Zuma now had to deal with Gordhan, who made it plain that he would maintain – even strengthen – the Treasury's political independence. He announced that he would not approve the SAA transaction and called for the appointment of a new board to clean up the carrier's financial affairs. He spoke out boldly against corruption and surged ahead with Treasury plans to bring transparency to bear on government contracts. All of this was anathema to Zuma, who had overplayed his hand and now faced an even more implacable guardian of the nation's finances.

By February 2016, Zuma was beginning to wear his irritation on his sleeve. Answering a question about his appointment of Van Rooyen, he said: 'That thing caused such havoc and people think Zuma just woke up one day and took a decision. You know Des van Rooyen is my comrade, MK for that matter, he's a trained finance and economic comrade and more qualified than any minister I have ever appointed in the finance issue.'[16]

The claim that Zuma was making political appointments at the behest of the Guptas to allow them to benefit unfairly from state resources gained ground. There were reports of cavalcades of ministerial vehicles coming and going from the Guptas' residence in Saxonwold – an amalgamation of several large properties surrounded by a high wall and patrolled by civilian security officers.

*

And so began a game of cat-and-mouse, with Zuma as the cat. The head of the Hawks, Major General Mathandazo Berning Ntlemeza, an out-and-out Zuma loyalist, announced on the eve of Gordhan's first budget speech that he was pursuing charges against Gordhan. These related to Gordhan's handling of the retirement of his deputy, Ivan Pillay, while he was head of SARS.

As speculation mounted that the country would witness the indignity of its Finance minister being arrested on the eve of his budget speech, Zuma met with Gordhan and his deputy, Mcebisi Jonas, and the presidential Twitter account published pictures of the men apparently enjoying each other's company: 'The minister and his team have done their best and the budget to be presented tomorrow on our behalf as Cabinet is good for the country and good for the economy. It's all systems go for budget,'[17] said Zuma. Once the budget speech had been delivered, the public outcry over Ntlemeza's 'charges' grew to a national clamour.

It was to be a long winter of discontent. Rumours swirled of an imminent Cabinet reshuffle, and the Presidency responded that these were not necessarily true, noting that the President had the power to reshuffle his cabinet 'at any time'. In May, Zuma again expressed his annoyance at being forced to back down on the appointment of Van Rooyen, telling the ANC in Gauteng: 'In December last year I appointed in the finance ministry a well-trained cadre of the ANC, Des van Rooyen, in the financial affairs [post]. He was the best candidate to take over the control of the economy. Instead, I was castigated worldwide, including by senior members of the organisation. I then realised I had touched the wrong nerve. South Africa is the only country in the world which does not control its own economy.'[18] Also in May, the Hawks spokesman Hlangwani Malaudzi said that although Gordhan had been sent questions, these were 'for clarity-seeking purposes, and never in our engagement in the media did we ever say that we are investigating the minister.'[19]

Just when relations between Gordhan, the Hawks and Zuma appeared to be thawing, the Hawks moved against him again on the eve of his medium-term budget speech. South Africa's Finance minister delivers this speech to sketch out a longer-term plan for government finances and economic activity. The Hawks asked Gordhan to appear before them for a 'warning statement'. Gordhan refused to do this, saying: 'I am advised by my legal team that the assertions of law made by the Hawks in their letter of August 21 2016 are wholly unfounded on any version of the facts. I, therefore, do not intend to present myself. I have a job to do in a difficult economic environment and serve South Africa as best I can. Let me do my job.'[20]

Again, Zuma was at pains to express his 'full support and confidence in the minister of finance'. But Zuma did add, through his spokesman Bongani Ngqulunga: 'The Presidency also wishes to emphasise that the president does not have any powers to stop any investigations involving any individual.'[21] Perhaps the cat knew the mousetrap was about to be sprung.

On the morning of 11 October 2016, the head of the NPA, Shaun Abrahams, called a surprise media briefing. He announced to a stunned national audience – the briefing was televised – that Gordhan, along with Pillay and his successor as head of SARS, Oupa Magashula, were charged on three counts related to 'misrepresenting to the government insurance fund and SARS that Pillay was entitled to full pension benefits whereas they knew well that severance package was not applicable to him'.[22] It seemed an extraordinary step to take over what appeared to be a routine human resources matter. Perhaps this is why Abrahams delivered the announcement in an uncomfortable staccato style, sounding like a man making his first public statement in a foreign language.

Gordhan chose to break with his traditional equanimity and issued a barbed statement: 'This is a moment when South Africans should really ask themselves, "Who are the Hawks, or these few people in the Hawks . . . Where do they get their political instructions from and for what purpose?" I intend to continue doing my job. The fight against corruption, maladministration and the waste of public resources will continue.'[23] A day later, Zuma again said that the country was 'anchored in the rule of law as well as fair and just judicial processes' and that Gordhan was innocent 'until and unless proven otherwise by a court of law'.[24]

It soon became apparent that Abrahams and Zuma had been playing political games by protesting that they were mere servants of the law. Two weeks or so after Abrahams made his staccato announcement, the *Sunday Times* revealed that he had met with Zuma and three Cabinet ministers 'behind closed doors' at the ANC's headquarters a day before announcing the charges. Abrahams protested that the Gordhan matter had not been discussed. He had made the trip to Luthuli House to discuss student unrest, he said, to a disbelieving nation.

Zuma went so far as to tell Parliament that, far from interfering, he was preventing the country from becoming a 'banana republic' by staying at arm's length from the matter. Again, there was national outrage. This time it was different. A broad swathe of South African society pledged its support for Gordhan. There could no longer be any pretence that the ANC was united. The ANC premier of Gauteng, David Makhura, spoke out in support of Gordhan, as did many struggle veterans and former justices.

All eyes turned to Ramaphosa.

From the time of his appointment as deputy president of the ANC and then of the country, Ramaphosa seemed to go out of his way to act as Zuma's loyal lieutenant, although this appeared to be done through gritted teeth. Even when Zuma was called to order by the Constitutional Court over the Public Protector's report on Nkandla, Ramaphosa had stayed out of the fray. His calculation appeared to be that the ANC tradition of projecting unity at all costs was so powerful that to contradict it would undermine his chances of one day succeeding Zuma. This tradition had been forged both in exile and inside the country when the movement adopted the practice of secrecy and a 'need-to-know' approach to counter the infiltration of the ANC by agents of the apartheid state. The concealment of political disagreements and a hard line against 'factionalism' were defences against one group's being played off against another to reduce the effectiveness of underground operations. The projection of unity and the downplaying of leadership ambitions became entrenched. When democracy arrived, these traditions remained in place within the ANC, although their usefulness was questionable.

Arguably, the ANC's decision to 'remain a liberation movement' and to reject the trappings of modern politics, such as open leadership contests and public honesty about disagreements, made it less able to operate effectively in the open democracy that was ushered in with the 1994 democratic election. Whatever its merits, this archaic approach continued to hold sway within the ANC decades into the democratic era. The only explanation for Rama-phosa's long silence on Zuma's abuses had to be that he calculated he could not break with this tradition and hope to remain a presidential contender.

But the blatantly political decision to charge Gordhan – a decision viewed by most legal observers as without legal basis and by political observers as a move to lever Gordhan out of the Finance ministry – was the straw that finally broke the camel's back. Ramaphosa crafted a statement in which he finally positioned himself outside of the Zuma camp. It was hardly a protest charter, and the wording suggested a political tightrope that Ramaphosa imagined existed somewhere in the ANC's political discourse: 'Events of the past few days regarding summonses served on Finance Minister Pravin Gordhan have been of concern to many South Africans across all sectors of society,' he began. 'As a member of the National Executive, I lend my support to Minister Gordhan as he faces charges brought against him by the National Prosecuting Authority. I have known and worked with Minister Gordhan both in government and during the days of the prosecution of the struggle for a non-racial, non-sexist democratic society. I therefore wish Minister Gordhan well as he prepares to deliver the Medium-Term Budget Policy Statement and hope that this challenge will not distract him from focusing on this important national task.'[25] Ramaphosa said he (he used 'we') respected 'the constitutional mandate that the NPA has to discharge without fear, favour or prejudice' but said this needed to be balanced against 'the right to be presumed innocent until proven guilty by a court of law'.

Although appearing to balance one side against the other, Ramaphosa also spoke of the need to defend the country's constitutional values: 'Accordingly, we must conduct ourselves in ways that will uphold our constitutional values and maintain South Africa's good reputation internationally.'[26] Although mildly worded and eminently defensible within the ANC as a statement of loyalty to a comrade facing troubled times, Ramaphosa's public announcement represented his first public break with Zuma, certainly to anyone who grasped its subtext – that the prosecution service was undermining the Constitution by targeting an innocent and admirable man. It sent a strong signal to the growing number of ANC leaders unhappy with Zuma that Ramaphosa stood with them, albeit at a remove occasioned by his serving at Zuma's pleasure in government.

*

South Africa is a country of political bombshells, and a large one exploded on the morning of Sunday 23 October 2016. The front page of the *Sunday Times* bore the headline 'Ajay Gupta "offered millions" to Jonas to "work with us"'. The Public Protector, Thuli Madonsela, was at the time compiling her report on so-called state capture, which considered high-level links between Zuma and the Gupta family, who had appointed his children to several high-profile positions and who were accused of wielding major influence over Zuma's decisions to the benefit of their business empire.

The *Sunday Times* article concerned revelations by Gordhan's deputy, Mcebisi Jonas, that he had been offered the Finance ministry by the Guptas during a meeting in 2015 at their compound in Saxonwold, Johannesburg. The essence of the story was that Ajay Gupta had offered Jonas R600 000 in cash in a black plastic bag and the job of Finance minister, as well as a further R600 million, to be paid in instalments, if he agreed to 'work with us'. The claim was alleged to have been contained in an affidavit to the Public Protector: 'Sources close to the probe said Jonas claimed in his affidavit that "work with us" meant he was expected to push for the approval of the nuclear procurement programme, estimated to be worth R1 trillion, and fire some Treasury officials who were critical of the programme.'[27]

The nuclear procurement programme was one of Zuma's pet projects. Against the advice of government's own strategists, who cautioned against an expensive nuclear build, Zuma had championed the rollout of a 'fleet' of nuclear power stations. The government had signed an agreement with Russia related to the construction and operation of the power stations, but this agreement was never made public, bypassing scrutiny by Parliament. The Gupta family had recently acquired a uranium mine, leading to further speculation that they would directly benefit from the nuclear programme by becoming a preferred supplier.

Critics of the nuclear proposal pointed out that it could cost more than R1 trillion, making future generations of South Africans slaves to a massive debt. And, they said, the cost of electricity generated by nuclear energy would be high if this was the mechanism that would be used to partially finance the programme.[28]

Gordhan had steadfastly refused to sign off on the nuclear programme, saying that a decision needed to be made in line with the country's financial capacity. This was widely read as a statement that South Africa quite simply could not afford the programme. Now, the *Sunday Times* article revealed, the Guptas had attempted to influence the decision on the nuclear build by trying to buy off Jonas.

Claims of Gupta interference in the executive were backed up by former government spokesman Themba Maseko, who revealed how Zuma had personally encouraged him to meet with the Guptas. At the meeting, Maseko said he was asked to spend government money on advertising in the Gupta-owned *New Age* newspaper. When Maseko refused a follow-up meeting, Ajay Gupta told him: 'I'm not asking you, I'm telling you.'[29] Maseko's failure to meet the Guptas' demands led to his being fired.

The ANC launched a probe into state capture. Like most ANC investigations of itself, this was to die a quick death, ostensibly because other agencies were probing the same thing. But it did encourage Ramaphosa to break cover. This was around the time that the Glencore deal with Oakbay was being finalised. Ramaphosa would have been all too aware of how state capture worked because of his previous association with Glencore as an empowerment partner.

He was still playing his 'inside' game and so used careful language that did not mention Zuma: 'The ANC is not for sale. Those who want to capture the ANC and make it their own and influence it to advance personal or corporate interest, you have come to the wrong address.'[30]

If Ramaphosa was coy about Zuma, he was prepared to go on the record about the Guptas: 'It is not only the Gupta family. There are a number of others as well, there are others who have either captured the state or are in the process of capturing the state, and we are saying to all and sundry, stop in your tracks, we are not going to allow you to capture this glorious movement, we will not allow that.'[31]

*

Gordhan delivered his medium-term budget statement to Parliament on 27 October. It was yet another forceful statement of his commitment to sorting out public enterprises and bringing order to government spending. As he spoke, Zuma fell asleep in his seat before the television cameras.

Not long after, Shaun Abrahams performed one of the most impressive political pirouettes of modern times. A few days after Gordhan's speech, he called another media briefing. The venue was packed with journalists wishing to capture the next instalment of the Gordhan drama. It was to be another extraordinary performance, although bereft of the comic grandeur and the staccato delivery that accompanied the announcement of charges. Abrahams began with a lengthy discourse about the law, pension funds and other miscellany before finally taking the plunge. With a whimper, the words came tumbling out: 'They did not have the requisite intention to act unlawfully. I have decided to overrule the decision to prosecute Mr Magashula, Mr Pillay and Mr Gordhan. I direct the summonses to be withdrawn with immediate effect.'[32] When asked if he would resign, Abrahams replied: 'Will I resign? Certainly not. Certainly not.' Following the farce, which had severely damaged the currency and the financial markets, the opposition DA brought a motion of no-confidence before Parliament.

South Africa's democratic Constitution offers two avenues for the removal of a sitting president. The first is impeachment. Section 89, 'Removal of President', states that the National Assembly 'with a supporting vote of at least two thirds of its members' may remove the president on the grounds of violating the Constitution or the law, serious misconduct or an 'inability to perform the functions of office'.[33] The consequences of such a removal are severe for the president, who may receive no benefits from that office or serve in public office in any capacity thereafter.

Intriguingly, though, the Constitution offers another method of removing the president in section 102, 'Motions of no confidence'. In terms of this section, a motion of no-confidence may be passed by a simple majority. This would require the president and members of the Cabinet to resign and for fresh elections to be called. In this scenario, the president could theoretically take his case to the people in an election and win back his office, although this would be unlikely in practice.

Because of the ANC's consistent hold on more than 60 per cent of the seats in the National Assembly, the opposition opted for the lower threshold of the vote of no-confidence, hoping to win the support of ANC MPs unhappy with Zuma to succeed. In the event, the no-confidence vote failed, except to demonstrate that Zuma and Gordhan had definitively parted ways. Gordhan was among 32 ANC MPs to abstain from voting after he notified the ANC Chief Whip that he would not attend the session.

The fall-out from the botched charging of Gordhan did not end there. It would play itself out inside the ANC, which discussed the matter at a meeting of its NEC on 29 November. At that meeting, the Minister of Tourism, Derek Hanekom, took the unprecedented step of calling for Zuma's recall from the presidency. Hanekom appeared to catch Zuma off-guard, and several of his allies flew in late to the meeting, which was extended by a day to accommodate the debate. Gordhan was among those who joined Hanekom in speaking out against Zuma. In the end, the NEC took no vote and did nothing, allowing Zuma to continue as president, though with his aura of invincibility somewhat tarnished.

The Christmas season arrived and an uneasy calm descended over the ANC and the country as Zuma and his detractors opted to stay behind their parapets. But once all were back in their offices in January, the rumour mill kicked back into life. Zuma, it was widely said, wanted Gordhan out and was merely waiting for the right moment to strike.

Gordhan prepared for his second budget speech since his re-appointment as Finance minister. Asked about the rumours, he said: 'The record is very clear about what we have delivered in the past 14 or 15 months and if the president chooses to redeploy us that's his decision. Words like "fire" . . . it is not very dignified. If the president chooses to redeploy us, as we say in the ANC, that is his prerogative . . . We have no appeal mechanism. We are very much alive to that situation.'[34]

On 23 February, Gordhan, flanked by Jonas, walked grimly over the cobbled paving to Parliament to deliver the budget speech. He had been asked whether he was going to be fired and had responded wearily that he served at the president's discretion. Inside the chamber, the ANC MPs rose to give him a standing ovation after the speech. Zuma, who joined in the standing ovation, shook his hand. But four ministers loyal to the president – Bathabile Dlamini (Social Development), Lindiwe Zulu (Small Business Development), David Mahlobo (State Security) and the man whom Gordhan had displaced after four days, Des van Rooyen (Cooperative Governance and Traditional Affairs)[35] – sat glumly on the government benches, refusing to applaud. Perhaps they knew that, as far as Zuma was concerned, Gordhan was a dead politician walking.

Then came the drama of March, when the conflict between Zuma and Gordhan finally reached its climax. Gordhan had left for the UK on the customary post-budget 'roadshow' designed to sell South Africa's financial credibility to foreign investors.

*

As rumours swirled that Zuma was preparing to act against Gordhan, the health of struggle veteran Ahmed Kathrada suffered a major setback. Kathrada had been Nelson Mandela's closest confidant and had shared decades of imprisonment with him on Robben Island. Kathrada had been in rude health for an 87-year-old, until he underwent surgery. As so often happens, one thing went wrong and then another. By the evening of Monday 27 March, Kathrada's foundation saw fit to warn the public that all was not well, stating that he had pneumonia. His condition had deteriorated and he was being kept comfortable. It was to be a week of high drama.

While the nation restlessly awaited news of Kathrada's fate, one man was otherwise preoccupied. In the Union Buildings, Zuma was putting the finishing touches to his plan to fire Gordhan and Jonas. Zuma took an extraordinary step on Monday afternoon: he ordered Gordhan, who had just stepped off the plane in London, to return home. And he instructed Jonas to cancel a similar trip to the US. Jonas was set to leave that evening. Speculation immediately mounted that Zuma was finally going ahead with the firing of the two. The financial markets reacted by hammering the rand, which had been at a 20-month high on Monday morning.

That evening, Zuma met with the ANC's top six – the structure with which he was obliged to share his Cabinet decisions since the Nenegate disaster of December 2015 – presumably to brief them on his plans. Ramaphosa, as ANC deputy president, was present. He heard Zuma out and aired his disagreement with the decision. The atmosphere was frosty.

Engagements were cancelled and Gordhan boarded a plane for South Africa on Monday evening. While he was in the air came the news that Kathrada had passed away. By the time Gordhan landed, the political reality of Kathrada's passing had dawned on Zuma.

Kathrada was no friend of the president. A year before, he had penned a blunt letter over Zuma's failure to abide by the Constitution and other failings, culminating with the sentence: 'Today I appeal to our president to submit to the will of the people and resign.' Kathrada was firmly in the ANC camp that wanted Zuma out.

Zuma knew that there would be a nationally televised funeral, which would turn into a pro-Gordhan rally if he were to proceed with his plan. So, having summoned Gordhan home urgently, he did nothing and said nothing. After landing, Gordhan said: 'The president is my boss so if he asks us to come back, we come back. There are many in government who want to do the right thing and make sure we keep our economy on track and keep our development moving in the right direction.' Asked about whether the move likely heralded a Cabinet reshuffle, Gordhan said: 'Let's wait and see.'

Gordhan then made his way to Luthuli House for a meeting. Afterwards he attended the Gauteng High Court in a case brought by him against Zuma's business associates, the Gupta family. Gordhan wanted the court to establish that he and other members of Cabinet were not in a position to intervene in decisions by a range of banks to close accounts linked to the Guptas because of suspicious transactions. Furious at the treatment of his friends, Zuma had formed a ministerial subcommittee to look into the banks' decision, and it would have to be disbanded if Gordhan won his case. Outside the courtroom, Gordhan told reporters he was, as far as he knew, still the Finance minister. Asked why he had been recalled, he said he had no idea and referred reporters to Zuma's office.

As Tuesday dragged on, speculation over Gordhan's fate continued and the rand was further weakened. South African bonds were battered. By Tuesday evening, it was estimated that the country's debt had grown by R2.6 billion in the day since Zuma's recall of Gordhan.

The president of the ANC usually played a leading role in the funerals of veterans, especially those held in as high regard as Kathrada was. But Kathrada's family told Zuma that he would not be given an opportunity to speak, a sign of their displeasure with his reign over Kathrada's beloved party. On Wednesday morning, Zuma issued a statement. After heaping praise on Kathrada, he concluded by saying that he would not attend the funeral service later that morning 'in compliance with the wishes of the family'.

It would fall to Cyril Ramaphosa to represent the government. Zuma was being petulant. He was free to attend the funeral, but had been asked not to speak. But it did offer Ramaphosa the opportunity to demonstrate that he had the support of those attending the funeral.

As the crowd gathered for the funeral service at Johannesburg's Westpark Cemetery, it was apparent that Zuma's fears were to be realised. It was to be a high-powered gathering of his critics and rivals. Former president Thabo Mbeki, whom he had removed from office, was present, along with former president Kgalema Motlanthe, who had stood against him unsuccessfully at Mangaung in 2012. Also present were Nelson Mandela's widow, Graça Machel, and his former wife, Winnie Madikizela-Mandela, an outspoken critic of Zuma. Then there was former ANC treasurer Mathews Phosa, who had also called on him to quit.

Ramaphosa took his seat in the front row, one seat away from Thabo Mbeki. The rivals put aside their history. They sat side by side, perhaps united by a common enemy. Also seated in the audience was the Chief Justice, Mogoeng Mogoeng, author of the scathing Constitutional Court judgment that had led to Kathrada's impassioned letter. Zuma had made it plain that he wanted his former wife, Nkosazana Dlamini-Zuma, recently returned from a bedraggled term as chairperson of the African Union Commission, to succeed him. She was also present.

Gordhan took his seat in the row behind the dignitaries. The master of ceremonies was Derek Hanekom, who had unsuccessfully proposed a motion to the NEC that Zuma be recalled. Seated in the front row in a light headscarf was Kathrada's widow, Barbara Hogan, herself a victim of a Zuma Cabinet reshuffle.

Hanekom introduced the first speaker, Gauteng premier David Makhura. The Gauteng region was opposed to Zuma and had also questioned his continuation as president, although it had subsequently muted its criticism. Makhura spoke of Kathrada as 'a man whose activism has been a consistent feature in the struggle for liberation', someone who had lived 'a rich life of purpose and sacrifice to humanity'.[36]

Kathrada and other veterans had requested a special consultative conference with the ANC leadership to discuss the state of the organisation and Zuma's presidency. This had been rebuffed by Zuma. Now Makhura said: 'We as leaders must have the humility to listen to stalwarts and veterans of our struggle. We must be angry if anyone insults our stalwarts and veterans.' There was loud applause.

Dlamini-Zuma had been touted by the Zuma faction of the ANC as a 'woman candidate' for the presidency. Now Hanekom asked the audience to acknowledge 'two powerful women', Madikizela-Mandela and Machel. They, he said, 'truly represent the best of women in South Africa'. The snub was palpable.

Cosatu's Bheki Ntshalintshali was the next to speak. He pointed out that he had 'never received any invitation to come here' as it was a funeral that anyone who honoured Kathrada was free to attend. It was a point about Zuma's absence: 'We must separate leaders from organisations. Leaders will come and go but the organisation will remain. Never for a moment understand that you are bigger than the organisation,' he said to applause.

He was followed by Blade Nzimande of the SACP, who put it more directly. Kathrada had passed, he said, 'at a time when parasitic patronage networks are seeking to capture our movement for their narrow interests. We say no to those intentions and we will continue to say no, no, no!' Again, there was loud applause.

Next to speak was the ANC's secretary general, Gwede Mantashe, who seemed strangely muted. He did say of Kathrada that 'he was incorruptible, not only in his politics but also in personal life. He was a man you knew could never let you down, never do something behind your back and never deceive you. You always knew where you stood with him.'

Finally, it was time for Motlanthe to deliver the eulogy: 'We should say it like it is. We are pained, gutted, saddened and sorrowful.

Each day of the enjoyment of freedom for all of us is the ultimate expression of gratitude to Comrade Kathy,' he said. Then he changed tack, saying: 'It would be disingenuous to pay tribute to the life of comrade Ahmed Kathrada and pretend that he was not deeply disturbed by the current post-apartheid failure of politics. In this regard we do not put words into his mouth posthumously. He penned a public letter to the president of our country in which he gave vent to his views about the state of the state.'

Then Motlanthe read from the letter: 'I have always maintained the position of not speaking out about any difference I harbour against my leaders and organisation, the ANC. The position of president is one that at all times must unite this country behind a vision and programme that seeks to make tomorrow a better day than today. It is a position that requires the respect of all South Africans.' He went on read Kathrada's plea to Zuma, 'that you will choose the correct way, that is, to consider stepping down'.

Applause erupted and then grew in volume. The mourners stood and cheered. In the front row, Ramaphosa – effectively represent-ing Zuma – and Mbeki remained seated. Mantashe folded his arms and leaned back, exchanging words with his deputy, Jessie Duarte.

When the applause had subsided, Motlanthe continued: 'Three hundred and forty days ago, Comrade Kathrada wrote this letter. His letter went without any formal reply.' Kathrada was, he said, protesting sleaze and corruption of the 'vilest' proportions. Motlan-the returned to his seat as the crowd stood and applauded.

Hanekom addressed Mantashe: 'Dear secretary general, the con-stitution of the ANC does not instruct us to unite the ANC, it instructs us to unite all the people of South Africa. When we go out of here inspired by our leaders, let us unite all the people of South Africa behind these noble goals, behind the vision of Ahmed Kathrada.'

There was one final gesture. Pravin Gordhan was asked to stand up from his seat in the middle of the hall. The message was clear.

He had the backing of those loyal to Kathrada's values. As the crowd cheered, he wiped tears from his face.

Then Zuma acted, announcing a Cabinet reshuffle that included the dismissal of Gordhan and Jonas and the elevation of Malusi Gigaba to the position of Finance minister. It immediately became apparent that Zuma had failed to properly consult the ANC's top six leaders before deciding on the reshuffle. The top six – Zuma, Ramaphosa, Mantashe, Duarte, Zweli Mkhize and chair Baleka Mbete – were supposed to collectively agree on such moves, in keeping with party policy that the president was required to consult the party on executive decisions.

The rift between Zuma and Ramaphosa finally burst out into the open. Ramaphosa stated publicly of Zuma's actions: 'He met with ANC officials. It was just a process of informing us of his decision. It was not a consultation because he came with a ready-made list.'[37] He went on to say: 'I raised my concern and objection on the removal of the Minister of Finance, largely because he was being removed based on an intelligence report that I believe had unsubstantiated allegations.'[38] The 'unsubstantiated allegations' referred to were apparently contained in this 'intelligence report' that suggested that Gordhan and Jonas were plotting with foreign forces to unseat Zuma. It was the sort of paranoia more typical of a military junta than an established democracy – though all too typical of Zuma's tenure – and the document aroused widespread scepticism.

By publicly breaking with Zuma over an executive decision for the first time, Ramaphosa had effectively thrown his hat in the ring. It was game on. From this point on, it would be a fight to the death – in the political sense, of course – between Zuma and Ramaphosa. Ramaphosa would finally allow his ambition to become president to rule over his more cautious side. Over the coming months, he would become more and more strident in his criticism of Zuma and state capture.

# NINE
## *To the front line*

I have to be prevented at all costs from ascending to the position
of president of the ANC. Some have even said it will happen
over their dead bodies. I have not committed any crimes, I have
not stolen any money, I have not looted state resources.
But I am being targeted and smeared. – *Cyril Ramaphosa*

The shifting of the political space against Zuma had been taking
place at a steady but glacial pace. Then it began to accelerate as
more and more evidence of his role in state capture began to
appear on the public record. One of the most significant contribu-
tions came in the form of a series of highly detailed and carefully
referenced articles, written under the pseudonym Lily Gosam.
These were published on the *Rand Daily Mail* website, of which
I was the editor.

Publication of the Lily Gosam articles presented me with one of
the most difficult decisions I ever had to make – and I had previously been editor of the *Sunday Times* and *The Times*, so I had no
shortage of experience with tough calls. I was being asked to publish articles exposing state capture by an anonymous contributor.
This was always going to be difficult in a partisan environment in
which the press was constantly accused by a vast array of 'Twitter
bots' – paid-for supporters of Zuma and the Gupta family – of
inventing fake news to wrongly implicate the president.

At the time, it was not widely known that there was an active
smear campaign against critics of the Guptas. Marketing strategist

Andrew Fraser would eventually expose the bots as nothing but an array of fake names that acted in concert to create the false impression that the public was unhappy with reporting on the Guptas. He found many of the bots were generated in India.[1]

But the content I was being offered was of such high quality – each paragraph contained two or three references to printed articles in the press or to other documents – and so compelling that I felt I had, for the first time, discovered the full and dirty truth of what was going on. After checking dozens of the references and finding them to be accurate, I was still not ready to publish. I insisted on speaking to the author directly and ascertaining his or her identity. What followed was an awkward conversation in which I probed the motives of the author. When I had satisfied myself that I was dealing with a bona fide writer with impeccable credentials, I agreed to go ahead and publish the articles under the Lily Gosam pseudonym.[2]

The articles joined the dots, fitting a seemingly disparate and disjointed string of events into a cohesive whole. Taken together, the articles explained that what was taking place in South Africa was nothing other than a well-planned strategy to loot the state by diverting resources from state-owned enterprises, such as Eskom and SAA, to companies linked to the Gupta family. Running parallel to this was a strategy to 'securitise' the democratic state by smearing critics of state capture, such as Public Protector Thuli Madonsela and members of the media, as agents of foreign powers.

On first reading the articles, I had to pinch myself. I had never been one to believe conspiracy theories, but these were not the ramblings of a paranoid victim. They were the academically sound, thoroughly referenced notes of someone who had obsessively followed every angle of the state capture story. The readership of the articles was vast – often greater than that of well-established columnists. In the end, the Twitter bots had their way and senior editorial voices began to systematically challenge the publication of the Lily Gosam articles because they might be caricatured as 'fake news'. They had a point. I relented and ended the series, which was, in any event, reaching its conclusion.

It would soon be clear that Lily Gosam had been right about everything she or he had written.

As Public Protector Thuli Madonsela's term of office drew to an end in October 2016, she made one final intervention that would have serious political repercussions. Madonsela had developed the habit of giving her reports dramatic titles. Her report on Jacob Zuma's abuse of public funds to expand his Nkandla homestead at the cost of R265 million had been called 'Secure in Comfort', a reference both to the excuse given – 'security' – and to the outcome – 'a more comfortable residence'.

In her final week in office, she released a long-awaited report entitled 'State of Capture', with a lengthy explanatory subtitle: 'Report on an investigation into alleged improper and unethical conduct by the President and other state functionaries relating to alleged improper relationships and involvement of the Gupta family in the removal and appointment of Ministers and Directors of State-Owned Enterprises resulting in improper and possibly corrupt award of state contracts and benefits to the Gupta family's businesses'.[3] This wordy explanation was followed by a more pointed quotation – from the judgment delivered in March 2016 by Chief Justice Mogoeng Mogoeng against Zuma in the Nkandla case. The quotation included Mogoeng's powerful phrase about the law being 'ready to chop the ugly head of impunity off its stiffened neck'.[4] The report was one last effort by Madonsela to live up to this expectation, and her findings would cast a new shadow over Zuma and those in his employ who were making executive decisions that enriched the Guptas and the Zuma family.

Among the matters Madonsela had investigated was Mcebisi Jonas's claim that he had been offered the position of Finance minister by the Guptas during a meeting at their Saxonwold residence. Jonas had issued an unprecedented – for a government minister – statement on how he had been approached by the Guptas: 'Members of the Gupta family offered me the position of Minister of Finance to replace then-Minister Nene. I rejected this out of hand. The basis of my rejection of their offer is that it makes a mockery of our hard-earned democracy, the trust of our people and no one apart from the President of the Republic appoints ministers.'[5]

Madonsela also investigated the following allegations, among others: that, during a meeting at the Saxonwold residence, and while Zuma was in the building, ANC MP Vytjie Mentor had been offered the post of Minister of Public Enterprises in exchange for cancelling an SAA air route, thus opening the door for a Gupta-linked airline; that the Gupta family had business dealings with government departments and state enterprises in which 'irregularities, undue enrichment, corruption and undue influence' may have occurred; and that Zuma had breached the Executive Code of Ethics by exposing himself to a conflict of interest and had failed to act in a manner consistent with his position.[6]

After interviewing witnesses – including a recalcitrant Zuma – and going as far as she could in the time she had, Madonsela summed up what she had concluded. It was, she said, 'worrying' that the Gupta family had been aware of developments surrounding the firing of the former Finance minister, Nhlanhla Nene, and that his replacement, Des van Rooyen, 'can be placed at the Saxonwold area on at least seven occasions including on the day he was announced as minister. This looks anomalous given that, at the time, he was a Member of Parliament based in Cape Town.'[7]

There followed a description of a series of incidents suggesting that Zuma had violated the Executive Code of Ethics, the rules of conduct prescribed by Parliament, which warranted further inquiry. Madonsela described how she had tried to get Zuma's co-operation but had failed to secure a meaningful response from him as he stonewalled her office.

She had written to him in March and asked him 'if you have any comments on the allegations leveled against you'. She received no response. In April, she wrote to him again and once more received no response. In September, she asked him for a meeting to afford him an opportunity to comment on the allegations. No response. In early October, she sent him notice of the complaints and detailed the evidence implicating him: 'I ended off the notice by advising the President that if I do not get his version which contradicts the said evidence, there would be a possibility that I could find that the above allegations are sustained by the evidence. I detailed the various conclusions that I would make in that case.'

Finally, a meeting was scheduled for 6 October. At this meeting, Zuma's legal team raised objections and asked for more time to study the documents and obtain advice. What then transpired was revealing: 'The President's legal advisor argued emphatically that the matter should be deferred to the incoming Public Protector for conclusion.' Zuma believed he would receive a better hearing from the new Public Protector, Busisiwe Mkhwebane, and the coming months would reveal why this was the case. The upshot of it all was that Zuma would subsequently object, to the point of cancelling a second meeting planned for 10 October. Mkhwebane announced the following year she was not so keen to look into state capture, preferring instead to lambast one of South Africa's largest banks, Absa, for apartheid-era loans, which she ordered it should pay back.

Madonsela turned to the behaviour of state functionaries, finding that Mineral Resources minister Mosebenzi Zwane's trip to Switzerland in December 2015, during which he assisted the Guptas in their acquisition of the Optimum colliery from Glencore, 'may not be in line with section 96(2) of the Constitution and section 2 of the Executive Members Ethics Act'. The Guptas' purchase of the Optimum mine, which Ramaphosa had once been associated with, was to become the central thread that, when unravelled, opened to public scrutiny just how state capture worked.

The nexus between Zwane's easing of the purchase of Optimum, which became part of Tegeta Exploration and Resources, and Eskom's subsequent decision to award it contracts and hand over money to the Guptas upfront exposed, in detail, how the crookery was being conducted. The awarding of contracts to Tegeta to supply the Arnot power station in Mpumalanga 'was made solely for the purposes of funding Tegeta and enabling Tegeta to purchase all shares in OCH [the Glencore company Optimum Coal Holdings] . . . The favourable payment terms given to Tegeta . . . need to be examined further.'[8] The Eskom board 'did not exercise a duty of care', which was a violation of the Public Finance Management Act.

Eskom's 'pre-payment' of R660 million to Tegeta in April 2016 was also suspect: 'Eskom held an urgent Board Tender Committee meeting at 21:00 in the evening to approve the prepayment.' 'Tegeta's conduct and misrepresentations made to the public with regards to the prepayment and the actual reason for the prepayment could amount to fraud. Furthermore, the shareholders of Tegeta (Oakbay, Mabengela, Fidelity, Accurate and Elgasolve) pledged their shares to Eskom in respect of the prepayment and thus knew of the nature of the transaction,'[9] Madonsela said.

What was astonishing about 'State of Capture' was Madonsela's carefully detailed account of the involvement of Eskom's CEO, Brian Molefe, in making the Optimum deal happen. The former

Transnet CEO was Zuma's most highly regarded operator in state-owned enterprises. Madonsela demonstrated, using cellphone records, that Molefe had been in frequent contact with the Gupta family and had been near their Saxonwold residence on numerous occasions. Molefe would subsequently deny this amid claims – made in jest – that he might have been visiting a shebeen in the area. The joke fell flat and Molefe was derided for his patronage of the 'Saxonwold shebeen'.

Madonsela found that 'between the period 2 August 2015 and 22 March 2016 Mr Molefe has called Mr Ajay Gupta a total of 44 times and Mr Ajay Gupta has called Mr Molefe a total of 14 times.'[10] It was plain to all that Molefe had behaved improperly, and he reacted to the release of the findings by resigning at a press conference where he burst into tears.

These were among many other findings of impropriety made by Madonsela. The punchline of the report was classic Madonsela. She quoted Zuma in an earlier case in which he said of the Nkandla matter: 'I could not have carried out the evaluation myself lest I be accused of being judge and jury in my own case.' Then she made her finding: 'The President to appoint, within 30 days, a commission of inquiry headed by a judge solely selected by the Chief Justice who shall provide one name to the president.' This judge, said Madonsela, had to be given 'the power to appoint his/her own staff and to investigate all the issues using the record of this investigation and the report as a starting point'.[11]

An all-out assault on Madonsela followed the release of the report. The Twitter bots labelled her an enemy of the struggle and an ally of 'white monopoly capital' – a term that would figure often in the months to come. But she was by no means alone in her analysis of what had gone wrong. As more and more information on the extent of state capture was placed on the public record, the pressure on Cyril Ramaphosa to take a stronger stand was growing.

In May 2017, a group of top academics, convened by Professor Mark Swilling of Stellenbosch University, produced the most comprehensive account of state capture to date. Under the title 'Betrayal of the Promise: How South Africa Is Being Stolen', Swilling and his colleagues laid bare the state capture machinery in vigorous detail. Among those on the panel were Professor Haroon Bhorat of the University of Cape Town's Development Policy Research Unit, Dr Mbongiseni Buthelezi and Professor Ivor Chipkin of the Public Affairs Research Institute at the University of the Witwatersrand, and Professor Mzukisi Qobo of the University of Johannesburg. The final contributor was 'Hannah Friedenstein', an independent journalist writing under a pseudonym. (I was immediately asked by my colleagues if this was Lily Gosam. I answered truthfully that I had absolutely no idea.)

The academics presented a cogent and compelling explanation for how state capture had evolved to become the country's single biggest threat: 'Until recently, the decomposition of South African state institutions has been blamed on corruption, but we must now recognise that the problem goes well beyond this. Corruption normally refers to a condition where public officials pursue private ends using public means. While corruption is widespread at all levels and is undermining development, state capture is a far greater, systemic threat. It is akin to a silent coup and must, therefore, be understood as a political project that is given a cover of legitimacy by the vision of radical economic transformation.'[12]

The shift of power away from the political process and into the backrooms where Zuma and the Guptas operated represented this 'silent coup': '[T]he task now is to expose and analyse how a Zuma-centred power elite has managed to capture key state institutions to repurpose them in ways that subvert the constitutional and legal framework established after 1994.'[13]

The post-apartheid state had sought to redirect resources to those who had been marginalised under apartheid, the report stated: 'Although significant progress was made, there is now widespread dissatisfaction across society and within the ANC itself with the performance of these institutions. Whereas the promise of 1994 was to build a state that would serve the public good, the evidence suggests that our state institutions are being repurposed to serve the private accumulation interests of a small powerful elite. The deepening of the corrosive culture of corruption within the state, and the opening of spaces for grafting a shadow state onto the existing constitutional state, has brought the transformation programme to a halt, and refocused energies on private accumulation.'[14]

The report went on to explain how this was occurring: 'The Gupta and Zuma families (popularly referred to as the "Zuptas") comprise the most powerful node, which enables them to determine for now how the networks operate and who has access. They depend on a range of secondary nodes clustered around key individuals in state departments, SOEs [state-owned enterprises] and regulatory agencies. In practice, this symbiosis is highly unstable, crisis-prone and therefore very difficult to consolidate in a relatively open democracy, as still exists in South Africa. It is much easier to consolidate in more authoritarian environments like Russia, which is why this kind of neopatrimonialism can quite easily drift into authoritarianism to consolidate the symbiotic relationship between the constitutional and shadow state thus reinforcing the current political crisis we face in South Africa.'[15]

*

As the evidence of state capture mounted, Ramaphosa's presidential bid got under way in earnest. In keeping with the times, it included a website and social media accounts. The site, ramaphosa. org.za, bore the title 'Cyril Ramaphosa 2017' (shortened to CR17

175

for social media) and used the black, green and gold colours of the ANC. Among the images on the home page was one of Ramaphosa with Nelson Mandela in which the former was holding high a copy of the Constitution. Both men were smiling. Superimposed on the image was a quotation from Ramaphosa: 'This is a moment for unity. This is a moment for renewal. It is a moment when we need to raise our gaze and look to a future that is better than yester-day and even much better than today.'

The slickly produced site included recent news reports on Ramaphosa, his speeches and a gallery of photographs of him crisscrossing the country on the campaign trail. It made a point of connecting with ANC tradition by means of tribute pages to ANC legends such as Oliver Tambo and Chris Hani. Ramaphosa was pictured with schoolchildren, inspecting an agricultural project alongside Trevor Manuel, and laying a brick at a construction site while wearing a white safety helmet.

Visitors to the site were invited to subscribe to the '#Siyavuma' newsletter. Issue 8 of 14 July carried an article entitled 'Reflections on the Policy Conference' and a tribute to the late ANC stalwart Emma Mashinini. The lead article on that day bore the innocuous title: 'Pursuing a National Democratic Society'.[16] 'Radical social and economic transformation must straddle all elements of eco-nomic activity and consistently improve the quality of life of all South Africans, especially the poor, according to delegates at the ANC's National Policy Conference,' the unnamed author wrote before getting down to the nitty-gritty: 'Delegates agreed that strengthening the ethical fibre of the state is critical not only to ensure its effectiveness, but to enhance its legitimacy in the eyes of society. This requires us to continually build and institution-alise the integrity, transparency, accountability and responsive-ness of the state machinery. Any form of state capture, by any segment of society, should therefore be condemned and combated, they said.'[17]

A second article dealt with the semantic victory of the Rama-phosa camp over the adjective 'white': 'In one of the most publi-cised debates at the ANC Policy Conference delegates broadly endorsed the description of the ANC's approach towards monopoly capital as one of "unity and struggle, cooperation and contesta-tion". This needs to be further discussed by the branches ahead of the 54th National Conference in December, and contrasts with the view of some formations that white monopoly capital should be declared the strategic enemy.'

*

The ANC's policy conference is a curious act of political theatre, taking place as it does some six months before the party's Decem-ber conference where leaders are elected. At the end of June 2017, the party's delegates gathered at Nasrec, an exhibition centre half-way between Soweto and central Johannesburg.

The atmosphere was heady. Not since 2007 had there been as public a battle for the leadership of the party. On that occasion, Jacob Zuma and Thabo Mbeki had tested their relative strength at the policy conference. Mbeki had mistakenly believed that he had the upper hand, but most observers of the policy conference knew that it signalled the likelihood that Zuma would defeat him that December.

Figuring out exactly who has the upper hand by observing the machinations at the policy conference requires a journalistic litmus test. At the 2017 policy conference, the litmus test was whether the adjective 'white' would be used to describe 'monopoly capital'. In the year leading up to the conference, the idea of 'white monopoly capital' had seemed to gain traction with some in the ANC, where it was used as a catch-all to describe the chief eco-nomic problem of the day – the stubborn persistence of economic inequality more than twenty years after the end of apartheid. But its origins were not entirely innocent.

President Jacob Zuma and Ramaphosa share a joke before the start of the ANC policy conference in June 2017. (Masi Losi/*Sunday Times*)

In May 2017, in a collaboration between various media houses and the amaBhungane investigative journalism unit, a massive trove of leaked Gupta emails – known as #GuptaLeaks – was made public, laying bare the structure of the family's business dealings. Once the Gupta emails began to reveal the inner workings of state capture, a curious fact emerged. The UK public relations company Bell Pottinger had been hired by the Gupta company Oakbay to polish up its image. Bell Pottinger had a reputation for embracing rogues in need of public repair. When the Dutch oil company Trafigura suffered a diminished reputation after the dumping of toxic waste in the port of Abidjan in 2006, whom did they call? Bell Pottinger. Other notable clients were the sex offender Rolf Harris, Syrian first lady Asma al-Assad and former Chilean dictator Augusto Pinochet.

Oakbay had been involved in scandal after scandal, particularly surrounding its acquisition of the Optimum coal mine. The company had also had its bank accounts closed by the major South African banks after a long list of suspect transactions were flagged by the government's Financial Intelligence Centre. But Bell Pottinger did not confine itself to merely writing press releases to burnish Oakbay's reputation. It emerged that the firm had played a role in a massive social media counter-offensive carried out by Gupta loyalists and reinforced by an army of fake social media accounts, the notorious Twitter bots, which spewed vitriol at those looking into state capture. In one of the most grotesque cases, an image of the well-respected former editor of City Press, Ferial Haffajee, was digitally manipulated to show her on the lap of Afrikaner billionaire Johann Rupert. Rupert, the bots loudly proclaimed, was in the vanguard of 'white monopoly capital', which sought to destroy the Guptas, who were on the side of 'radical economic transformation' – the other phrase that would dominate discussion at the policy conference.

The ANC, with its tradition of non-racialism, had often spoken about the persistence of racial inequality in the post-apartheid era. But the party had been cautious about assigning racial slurs to its policy concepts because it accepted that South Africans of all races were legitimate citizens of the country. The 'white monopoly capital' smears were crude attempts to mobilise on the basis of race and were not accepted by many within the party.

At the policy conference, the subject of whether the party ought to use the adjective 'white' became a hot topic for debate. It was plain that many of the ministers and officials who were identified with the Gupta family and Zuma's faction wanted the term to be used, while party traditionalists were dead against it. In the end, the idea was defeated in 9 of the conference's 11 commissions.

In a report-back on the conference, the ANC's Joel Netshitenzhe, a leading intellectual under Thabo Mbeki but sidelined by Zuma, explained what had happened: 'There was then an intense discussion on the issue of "monopoly capital" and the outcome of that discussion is as follows: Firstly, it reiterates what is contained in the 2007 strategy and tactics document. And this is that the relationship between the ANC and monopoly capital in particular, but also capital in general, is one of unity and struggle or, if you like, cooperation and contestation.

'There are areas where we would seek to cooperate with them – higher rates of investment, job creation, skilling of people, matters to do with broad-based black economic empowerment and so on. But there is also the challenge of monopoly companies conducting themselves in such a way that they undermine societal interests – collusion, high prices in the product markets, high returns that would not reflect the correct or appropriate distribution of income between the managers and the workers ...

'The issue was then raised: do we want to characterise monopoly capital as it manifests itself in South Africa as "white" monopoly capital, and nine out of those 11 commissions said the phenomenon of monopoly capital is a global one and it manifests itself differently in various parts of the globe, and in that context, it would therefore not be correct to characterise ours simply as "white monopoly capital".'[18]

The signal was clear: the Zuma camp, despite months of public relations propaganda, had failed to win the policy debate. The ANC maintained the fiction that there was no open campaigning for the presidency just yet, but, reading the political tea leaves, it was clear Ramaphosa was now gaining the upper hand in the fight to succeed Zuma. On 12 July 2017, Ramaphosa moved his campaign into overdrive.

By now, Zuma had become so toxic within the Tripartite Alliance of the ANC, SACP and Cosatu that the SACP joined Cosatu in stating that he was no longer welcome at their official events.

With Zuma out of the picture, it fell to Ramaphosa to address the SACP's congress in Boksburg on 12 July. He did not mince his words. Whereas in the past he had carefully hedged his statements, he now spoke out directly about 'rampant corruption that is spilling out in emails':[19] 'Even as delegates gathered to deliberate on these issues, more and more information was emerging about the extent to which our state-owned enterprises have been looted, how individuals in positions of responsibility have benefited from actions that are, at best, unethical and, at worst, criminal. There is not a day that passes that we do not gain greater insight into a network of illicit relationships, contracts, deals and appointments designed to benefit just one family and their associates. We cannot turn a blind eye to these revelations.'[20]

Whereas he had spoken previously of the need for investigations to reveal whether the state capture allegations were true, he now said: 'We now know without any shred of uncertainty that billions of rands of public resources have been diverted into the pockets of a few.' Ramaphosa said that an 'independent' commission of inquiry into state capture was needed. This had been one of Thuli Madonsela's recommendations in the 'State of Capture' report, though with the twist that the Chief Justice would appoint the commissioner. After several months of prevarication, the new Public Protector, Busisiwe Mkhwebane, supported Madonsela's finding, breaking with her initial refusal to directly challenge Zuma and the Guptas.

Ramaphosa now appeared to back this up, saying, 'As the revolutionary democratic movement, as the Alliance, we need to draw a line in the sand. We need to mobilise our structures and our supporters to oppose state capture and corruption in whatever form it takes. We need to send a clear message that we will not protect those within our ranks who are involved in such activity.'[21] The last statement was significant. It signalled that Ramaphosa was laying to rest speculation that he might offer Zuma the prospect of a pardon in exchange for smoothing his path to the presidency. Finally, he offered a vision of hope: 'Our people are watching in fear, wondering if we are still capable of leading them. They hear in our language, in our ideas, a hankering after past victories and past glory – yet they long most of all to hear about the future.'[22] A line had indeed been drawn in the sand. It was to be a fight to the bitter end.

\*

In November 2016, Ramaphosa's campaign for the ANC presidency received a major boost when Cosatu, his old trade union federation, announced that it would back him. The federation's general secretary, Bheki Ntshalintshali, stated: 'We are asking our members [who are also members of the ANC] to consider in their nomination deputy president Ramaphosa to succeed the president . . . We shall work to lobby and influence the ANC structures to support cadre Cyril Ramaphosa as the next leader of the movement.'[23]

The federation's support for Ramaphosa was not guaranteed, however, as Zuma had devoted much energy to winning it over to his camp. When he was contesting the presidency with Thabo Mbeki in 2007, Zuma had received strong backing from Cosatu, and its then general secretary, Zwelinzima Vavi, had gone so far as to liken Zuma's campaign to a 'tsunami'. Vavi subsequently changed his mind and admitted he had been wrong to back Zuma and the 'hyenas' who were behind corruption in government. In November 2014, Cosatu voted to expel the National Union of Metalworkers of South Africa (Numsa) from the federation after the union refused to support the ANC during the election campaign that year. Vavi supported Numsa's view that the ANC did not deserve union support while Zuma was in office, and he was also expelled in March 2015. He went on to form a rival structure, the

South African Federation of Trade Unions (Saftu). The departure of Numsa and the continuing decline of the NUM left Cosatu in a greatly weakened state and more dependent than ever on public-sector workers, whose unions now constituted the largest component of its membership.

Cosatu's president, Sdumo Dlamini, made several public pronouncements in favour of Zuma, creating the impression that the federation supported the president's faction within the ANC. But the federation's leadership turned its back on Zuma's preferred candidate to succeed him – his former wife, Nkosazana Dlamini-Zuma – and instead backed Ramaphosa.

Cosatu's support for Ramaphosa was significant given the criticism he had received over the Marikana massacre. The federation's second deputy president, Zingiswa Lozi, in response to a question from a journalist, signalled that Cosatu would work to distance Ramaphosa from Marikana: 'There are many things that follow an individual, but you keep raising the issue of Marikana although a commission never found Cyril guilty of any wrongdoing. Issues would continue to be raised . . . never mind who leads the ANC. The war is not against the individuals, but against the ANC.'24 First deputy president Tyotyo James said, 'If you look at the history, how the deputy president was one of the founders of the NUM and subsequently its founding secretary, you need not ask no more. He took mine workers out of the worst situations they faced at the time. He also played a very important role in the drafting of this country's constitution.'25

Ramaphosa sealed the union federation's support when he addressed its central committee in May 2017. Such an address would normally be made by the ANC president, but Cosatu's leadership stated explicitly that it would not allow Zuma to address it. Ramaphosa's address was that of a man at ease with his surroundings. He jokingly referred to Gwede Mantashe's 'beard that continues to grow greyer and greyer, largely because of the challenges and the problems that he faces in the African National Congress'. Ramaphosa went out of his way to heap praise on Cosatu, 'the most revolutionary of trade union federations we've got in our country . . . you are still the biggest and you are still the strongest, that you must believe.'[26]

Also in May, the South African National Civic Organisation (Sanco), the largest agglomeration of community organisations in the country, endorsed Ramaphosa. General secretary Skhumbuzo Mpanza made a plea for unity: 'We therefore can't afford a situation whereby the ANC is shaken in the upcoming elections and we can't witness a time in our history where again our society is leaderless. We therefore believe that the most feasible way to retain unity and cohesion in our movement is to allow the current deputy president of the ANC to ascend to ANC president in the upcoming national conference in December.'[27]

In June, the Gauteng ANC chairman, Paul Mashatile, also endorsed Ramaphosa, saying, 'Our people will never abandon the ANC if we do the right thing. But they cannot continue to support us if we deviate. It's important that our message [be] very clear that we will get the ANC back onto its right path.'[28] The Gauteng ANC had been openly critical of Zuma's presidency, and had spoken out publicly against him after he was found to have violated the Constitution over Nkandla.

Buoyed by the flow of endorsements, Ramaphosa used his speech to the SACP congress to express with growing clarity his public rejection of Zuma, and to give shape to a social democratic vision. His core constituency was Cosatu, and his supporters were, for the most part, to the left of the ANC centre. Now he called on the SACP to 'weave together the revolutionary democratic, socialist and trade union strands of the broad liberation movement into a tight alliance of formations that share a common approach towards the National Democratic Revolution and its objectives.'[29]

*

In August 2017, the campaign for the ANC presidency took a nasty turn. It all began when reports surfaced that the Deputy Minister of Higher Education, Mduduzi Manana, had beaten a woman outside a nightclub in Fourways, Johannesburg. Manana admitted to the assault, saying he had been heavily provoked. No action was taken against him within the ANC until the public outcry reached boiling point and he stepped down. Amid celebrations to mark Women's Month, pressure mounted on the ANC Women's League to denounce Manana and convince the authorities to act against him.

But, instead of taking up what appeared to be a clear case of abuse, the leader of the Women's League, Social Development minister Bathabile Dlamini, prevaricated. The controversial Dlamini, an ardent supporter of Zuma and his chosen successor, Nkosazana Dlamini-Zuma, hinted darkly that certain ANC leaders were guilty of worse abuse and it would be pointless to act against Manana while they remained untouched: 'Any ANC leader who wants to lead the ANC with female members must straighten up . . . There is blood dripping in their bedrooms because they abuse their partners.'[30] She refused to name the 'abusers'.

Eventually, it was the EFF's Julius Malema who placed a name in the public domain. In an interview with Capricorn FM, he said: 'Let me tell you why Bathabile [Dlamini] says there are worse people than Mduduzi Manana in the ANC. She is referring to Cyril Ramaphosa; they are saying he used to beat up his wife.'[31]

It was a bombshell. Ramaphosa had been blamed for the Marikana massacre and had been accused of cosying up to 'white monopoly capital', but this was an allegation of an altogether different character. It was personal and it was intended to severely damage his support within the ANC, particularly among women.

His former wife, Hope Ramaphosa, immediately spoke out against the claim, saying, 'I lived with him, and had opportunity to make him angry many times, but never ever did Cyril lift a finger. Cyril would rather negotiate or do things amicably than beat them up. I was his wife and girlfriend for a very long time, Cyril would not beat up a woman. He is very sensitive to women's issues.'[32] Ramaphosa's son Andile also dismissed the allegation in a social media post.

The former governor of the South African Reserve Bank, Tito Mboweni, rushed to Ramaphosa's defence, posting on Facebook: 'I warned in May that this ANC Leadership thing is going to get nasty. Smear campaigns will destroy this organization. I do not believe for a moment that my brother and comrade has ever, ever, raised his hand against his wife. Ever, never! I think people must debate policy and ability, capacity and capability to lead the ANC and South Africa. We are a complex society, economy and politics. We need a leadership that can comprehend, integrate complex challenges, provide solutions and lead. We don't need smear campaigns a la Bell Pottinger. If I am wrong on this, God help us.'[33]

Ramaphosa's CR17 online supporters' network also dismissed the charge: 'With the high levels of domestic violence in South Africa, it is extremely unfortunate that baseless rumours of this nature are used for political gain.' The campaign warned of the 'destructive role that fake intelligence reports have played in our public life' and urged journalists to treat such reports with caution. The campaign went further and said it supported 'the thorough investigation by appropriate authorities of any and all credible allegations of criminal activity, especially violence against women and allegations of misappropriation of public funds'.[34]

The outright dismissal of the charge by Ramaphosa's wife

suggested that the allegation was an unfounded smear intended to hurt him politically. There was more to come.

*

As December approached, the campaign against Ramaphosa grew desperate. He had been warned by some inside the intelligence establishment that a smear campaign was being prepared around allegations that he was a 'womaniser'. Ramaphosa had had an affair, which he had disclosed to his wife, who had forgiven him.

On 3 September, the *Sunday Independent* newspaper published a salacious front-page article under the headline 'Ramaphosa "The Player"'. Ramaphosa had tried to interdict the newspaper against publishing the story but had failed. The judge said he had not proved the case was urgent. The newspaper's editor, Steven Motale, was an unapologetic supporter of President Jacob Zuma. The previous week, the newspaper had carried an article arguing that Ramaphosa ought not to be president because he could face 'mass murder charges' over Marikana at any time. Seamlessly blending editorial comment and reporting, the article was written by the editor himself.

The 'exposé' claimed that Ramaphosa had had many affairs, which disqualified him from standing for president because his 'presidential campaign is modelled on moral and ethical leadership'. Ramaphosa, it said, 'appears not to practice what he preaches'.[35] The newspaper claimed to have documents linking Ramaphosa to eight women and promised a series of exposés over several weeks. The woman the article focused on appeared to be the woman that Ramaphosa had told his wife about. Others flatly denied having affairs with him.

The newspaper's campaign against Ramaphosa appeared to be in overdrive. The main feature article in its 'Dispatches' section bore the headline 'State capture is a hokum argument', and an editorial comment piece on mining carried the byline of Mosebenzi Zwane, the Gupta-linked Mineral Resources minister.

Ramaphosa responded angrily to the claims made by the *Sunday Independent*. In an interview with the *Sunday Times*, he said that the other seven women named in the 'exposé' were students he and his wife, Tshepo Motsepe, were assisting financially: 'I am not a blesser. My wife and I support 54 young people every month – 30 females and 24 males. We are transforming people's lives.'[36] Motsepe said, 'It is very sad what is happening. It's disappointing that people have to go to such lengths to discredit a person. I am very, very upset about it. We have been together for a very long time and are happily married. I support and respect him and I love him.'[37]

Ramaphosa told the *Sunday Times* that he believed he was the victim of a campaign to prevent him becoming president 'at all costs': 'I have to be prevented at all costs from ascending to the position of president of the ANC. Some have even said it will happen over their dead bodies. I have not committed any crimes, I have not stolen any money, I have not looted state resources. But I am being targeted and smeared. Basically, state institutions have been utilised to hack into my private emails. State institutions should never be used to fight political battles.'[38] He had been warned that 'they are building a file on me, that [the campaign] would even go on to be violent. They are going to get desperate.'[39]

The Sunday after the news broke, a ripple of activity by those supportive of the Guptas unfolded. The Gupta news channel, ANN7, reported on an ANC Youth League statement calling on Ramaphosa to restore the party's good name. In KwaZulu-Natal, Ramaphosa's rival, Nkosazana Dlamini-Zuma, happened to find herself at a women's rally. Ramaphosa himself addressed branches of the ANC's West Rand region. When he spoke of state resources being used to smear him because he was running for the presidency, he received the loudest cheer of the day.

The *Sunday Independent*'s promise of a series of further exposés in the weeks after the infidelity article fizzled out. Instead, the newspaper appeared to backtrack the following week, affording Ramaphosa the opportunity to state his case on the front page.

*

As the December conference grew ever closer, Ramaphosa's resolve appeared to be growing. He had started out as a Zuma 'insider'. Now he was an outsider, fighting against a system that appeared to be wholly directed at thwarting his political ambitions. Should his campaign to become ANC president and then president of the country in 2019 succeed, Ramaphosa would finally have the opportunity to clear out the rot.

The defining battle of his political life loomed. The scene would be the ANC elective conference at Nasrec. It would all come down to whom the 5 000 ANC voting delegates would choose as their new president.

# TEN

# Turbulent ascent

It gives us a beachhead – a beachhead to be able to start the process of reinstilling the values of our movement in the ANC and hoping that people will embrace that. – *Cyril Ramaphosa*

Cyril Ramaphosa was celebrating his 65th birthday with a party at the FNB Conference Centre in Sandton in late November 2017. Except that it wasn't just a birthday party. It was also the occasion of the launch of his book *Cattle of the Ages*. And it was a gathering of the faithful in the final stretch of his campaign to become president of the ANC.

The list of invited guests included Cabinet ministers fired by Jacob Zuma, among them Blade Nzimande, the SACP boss who had been dropped from the Higher Education portfolio after he and his party openly called for Zuma's removal. Also present was Pravin Gordhan, whom Zuma had dismissed as Finance minister in the most controversial move of his presidency. They mingled with the struggle and business elites. Colin Coleman, who had been a student activist and an administrator at the constitutional negotiations, was present. He was now the head of Goldman Sachs in South Africa.

The cover of Ramaphosa's book depicts two bulls. Their impossibly large horns point up to the sky like inverted McDonald's arches. From the podium, Ramaphosa told the story of how he had obtained the herd. The audience was rapt as a gripping tale of biotech innovation, power and influence unfolded.

Ramaphosa was in Uganda when he was struck by the sight of a herd of Ankole cattle belonging to that country's president, Yoweri Museveni. Their horns were hollow, and when the animals walked together, the horns knocked against each other, producing a unique other-worldly sound, according to those who heard them.

Ramaphosa wanted to bring some of the animals to his South African game farm, Ntaba Nyoni, but South African agricultural officials were having none of it. The disease risk was too high. Undeterred, Ramaphosa purchased a selection of the cattle from Museveni (at the knock-down price of $200 a head) and trucked them over the border to Ol Pejeta in Kenya. There, the herd grazed in the shadow of Mount Kilimanjaro, their tranquil existence occasionally interrupted by the 'flushing' of embryos.

A South African veterinarian, Morné de la Rey, who had previously cloned a cow, was now working on cloning an entire herd. The harvested embryos were transported to De la Rey's Embryo Plus facility in Brits. In the laboratory, they were 'tricked' into believing they had been fertilised. A herd of Ankole cattle emerged from the test tubes and were soon grazing on Ramaphosa's farm. This herd now numbers over a hundred beasts.

Photographer Daniel Naudé was hired to document the development of the herd. He followed the cattle around – a pursuit not without its dangers. Although the breed is not aggressive by reputation, it would take only mild annoyance for one of those horns to cause serious damage.

One of the speakers that evening was ANC secretary general Gwede Mantashe. He said he needed to be around Ramaphosa to bring him under control when his 'Scorpio' emerged. These were flashes of anger that needed to be headed off before they became destructive. Mantashe's reference to Ramaphosa's politics broke the spell, reminding guests that the ANC's elective conference was barely two weeks away.

When Ramaphosa rose to speak, there was loud cheering. His speech was classic Ramaphosa, a mixture of humour and deadly serious politics. He acknowledged his Cabinet colleagues and then drew a laugh by referring to 'former Cabinet colleagues' Nzimande and Gordhan. He acknowledged Ankole breeders Jacques Malan and Nico Oosthuizen, and quipped: 'If you never thought I'm ambitious, I'm hugely ambitious. I am going to become president of the Ankole Breeders Society.'[1]

The Ankole were known in Uganda as the 'Cattle of the Kings', but he had decided to call his book *Cattle of the Ages* to avoid the 'elitism' associated with royalty. He announced plans to give 20 of the cows to farmers and 20 more to workers: 'The proceeds are going into a trust fund which will help fund the education of their children.' He said he wanted to start an incubation centre for small farmers.

Then the tone of the evening changed as Ramaphosa raised a deadly serious political matter: 'Land still is a big challenge in our country. I call it the original sin. The dispossession of land led to poverty and led to inequality that we have. As a country, we are still burdened by this terrible inequality that we inherited from centuries of colonialism and apartheid. We cannot continue with a situation like this. As I'm an actor in farming, I find that many of our people, black people, are eager to get into farming, they want to become successful farmers. What holds them back is access to land.'

The Constitution negotiated in 1996 had presumed that the cut-off point for land claims would be 1913, the year the pernicious Natives Land Act had been passed by the Union Parliament, severely limiting black ownership of land. Ramaphosa made an admission: 'When we drafted the Constitution, somehow there was a sleight of hand where people thought 1913 onwards was what we need to focus on. But, truth be told, very little land was taken away from our people from 1913. What happened after 1913 were just some removals. The real act of dispossession was before 1913, so it has to be addressed. That would seem to double our problems and difficulties when it comes to land. We need to sit back and think about this because on a daily basis we find land hunger to be an issue that people want to be addressed.'

Ramaphosa was sending two clear signals: he might be one of the architects of the Constitution, but he was open to changing it on the land question; and he might be a powerful landowner, but he identified strongly with the landless.

It was a sobering message for those who believed Ramaphosa would take a moderate approach to what the ANC had begun to call 'radical economic transformation' once he was elected president. Ramaphosa's view on the injustice of land dispossession was not something he was conveniently going along with. It was a deeply held view that he would take with him on his journey to the presidency.

*

As the ANC's December conference approached, a frenzy of speculation erupted about who would win. There were several candidates for president, but it boiled down to a two-horse race between Ramaphosa and Nkosazana Dlamini-Zuma. The latter, a former wife of Jacob Zuma, was clearly his first choice as successor. She had the support of ministers known to be aligned with Zuma and the Gupta family, such as Mosebenzi Zwane, Bathabile Dlamini and Des van Rooyen.

The mathematics of the ANC conference appeared simple: the winner would need the support of a majority of the just over 5 000 voting delegates. But the reality was more complex. The delegates were mandated to vote one way or the other by the branches, but nothing stopped them from ignoring this and voting for someone else during the conference's secret ballot. Before the conference, branches declared their support for one or another candidate and it was possible to begin speculating over who was in the ascendency. There were, however, just over a thousand branch votes that were not 'declared' one way or another – enough to skew the outcome of the vote.

Ramaphosa had the support of five of the ANC's nine provinces – Eastern Cape, Gauteng, Limpopo, Northern Cape and Western Cape – while his rival was supported by four provinces – Free State, KwaZulu-Natal, Mpumalanga and North West. But this was by no means the full picture.

One of Ramaphosa's smartest moves had been to concentrate his effort on Zuma's home province of KwaZulu-Natal. Although he did not have the majority of branches, he had managed to split the province and held almost a third of the votes.

But the biggest imponderable was Mpumalanga, whose premier, David 'DD' Mabuza, was a Machiavellian power player. More than half of Mpumalanga's delegates – some 468 in total – had voted for neither Ramaphosa nor Dlamini-Zuma, declaring themselves in favour of 'unity'. With the election looking too close to call, Mabuza's 400 votes held the balance of power.

The conference was due to start on 16 December, South Africa's Day of Reconciliation holiday, at Nasrec. Thousands of delegates queued up for accreditation, and it soon became apparent that there was no way the conference would start on time. A battle over exactly who would be accredited ensued as the December sun beat down on the restless delegates.

Behind closed doors, a momentous decision was being made. On the eve of the conference, three court judgments were issued concerning the legitimacy of delegates in three provinces. After much debate, the party decided to disqualify 16 branches from KwaZulu-Natal, four from Gauteng, 38 from North West and a further 14 from the Free State. A further 52 provincial executive delegates from KwaZulu-Natal and the Free State were refused voting rights.

The decision favoured Ramaphosa. North West, KwaZulu-Natal and the Free State were provinces that supported Dlamini-Zuma, and only four branches from Gauteng, which supported Ramaphosa, had been barred from voting.[2] In addition, not all delegates turned up for the conference, so the voting delegate count dropped from 5 186 to 4 776. Spreadsheets were adjusted. With the Mpumulanga 'unity' vote out of the equation, the result was impossible to predict. My spreadsheet showed Ramaphosa had fallen behind by a small margin, but there was a lot of guess-work involved.

The conference finally got under way. Zuma gave his final speech as ANC president. It served as a reminder to all – perhaps even to his supporters – of why he had to go. That very morning, he had unilaterally announced the introduction of state-funded free higher education, contradicting the recommendations of a commission he had asked to investigate the matter, and surprising the ANC leadership and the Treasury, which was still discussing what the country could afford.

It was an unashamedly populist move, aimed at bolstering his camp's position on the eve of the conference. Zuma's address, delivered with his trademark hesitant staccato, was less a speech than an attempt to cast himself as a successful president nobly exiting the stage after a decade of benign rule: 'The fact that you gave me this responsibility – I would like to thank you and humble myself and say, I tried my best.'

Zuma was adamant that he would support whoever emerged as the new ANC president: 'Standing here, I'm waiting for one leader whom I'm going to call my president.' But he desperately wanted Dlamini-Zuma to win. In October, the Supreme Court of Appeal had upheld an earlier ruling by the Gauteng High Court to reinstate over 700 counts of corruption and fraud against Zuma dating back more than a decade. Zuma needed a president who would pardon him in the event that he was convicted.

In what appeared to be an effort to dilute a possible Ramaphosa victory, Zuma proposed that there be two deputy presidents,[3] a proposal that was shot down by delegates. Word began to circulate that Mabuza had broken with the Zuma camp.

Ramaphosa had in early November surprised everyone by announcing a 'slate' of leaders for the party's top six positions. He named Naledi Pandor, a smart and effective Cabinet minister with a low profile in the ANC, as his candidate for deputy president. The message was clear – someone else could easily take this position.

Finally, on the evening of 17 December, delegates began voting for the top six positions. Eerie nocturnal meetings of the opposing factions took place, accompanied by the strains of freedom songs. It was not unlike an ancient Greek battlefield, with the light coming from cellphone screens rather than burning torches.

The voting continued on the morning of 18 December as several prominent leaders announced they had voted for Ramaphosa. Among them were the party's national spokesperson, Zizi Kodwa, and its chief whip in the National Assembly, Jackson Mthembu.

Finally, on the evening of 18 December, the results of the election were announced. The nation tuned in to a live television broadcast to hear that Ramaphosa had defeated Dlamini-Zuma by 2 440 votes to 2 261, a margin of just 179 votes. It was the narrowest victory for an incoming leader in the party's history. The division was plain to see as half the hall erupted in raucous applause while the other half sat in stunned silence. On the streets of nearby Soweto, there was celebration.

Then the rest of the top six were announced. Ramaphosa supporters Gwede Mantashe (chairman) and Paul Mashatile (treasurer general) had won. But there were other powerful figures outside of Ramaphosa's circle alongside whom he would have to steer the organisation. David Mabuza's plan paid off and he was elected party deputy president, while Free State premier Ace Magashule, a strong Zuma supporter, was given the powerful secretary general position. Jessie Duarte, also associated with Zuma, would continue as deputy secretary general.

Ramaphosa was president, but he did not have a free hand. He would have to accommodate his opponents or face accusations that he was acting without a mandate from the leadership.

There would be one more twist to the fraught election. Magashule's triumph over Ramaphosa's preferred candidate, Senzo Mchunu, was questioned when it came to light that over 68 votes had not been counted. Naturally, rumours circulated that the fix was in. Eventually Ramaphosa defused the situation. He met with his supporters at a caucus meeting to discuss the missing votes. One of those present recorded Ramaphosa as saying, 'We must not allow the conference to degenerate into controversy and legal suits that will nullify the result that we've come up with.'

Then he went back to one of his favoured metaphors: 'What this does, notwithstanding the fact that it may not be what we all wanted, it gives us a beachhead – a beachhead to be able to start the process of reinstilling the values of our movement in the ANC and hoping that people will embrace that. And I have no doubt that the majority of our members want an ANC that subscribes to the values that are set out in our Constitution, the values of the founding fathers and mothers of our movement.'[4]

The party commissions reported back on the resolutions put before the conference. Grabbing most attention was the decision that the Constitution be amended to allow for the expropriation of land without compensation. The decision followed a scuffle on the conference floor as delegates disagreed on the wording. While commentators read this as a defeat for Ramaphosa, it was, in fact, in keeping with what he'd said at his birthday party.

There was also a resolution supporting Zuma's announcement of free higher education and another calling for the 'nationalisation' of the Reserve Bank, which, although a public institution, still has private shareholders (who have no influence on policy). The party was tilting in a populist direction, and Ramaphosa would have to go with it or face isolation in the leadership.

There was bad news for Zuma. The conference resolved that he should report to the ANC leadership on his decisions as president of the country. And, he was to appoint a judicial commission of inquiry into state capture immediately. Zuma had wanted to broaden the commission to look at all instances of state capture over many decades, but the conference decided it should follow the narrow recommendations of the previous Public Protector, who had focused on Zuma's administration.

*

Finally, the moment arrived and Ramaphosa rose to give his first speech as ANC president. Taking to the stage to read from an iPad, Ramaphosa pitched for unity: 'In recent times, we have seen the ANC at its worst. We have seen an organisation divided against itself. And yet we have also seen glimpses of the ANC at its best. Over the last few days, we have seen the ANC that we know and love.'

He pledged a change in the way that the ANC went about its business: 'We are resolved to be a more responsive and more accountable leadership and movement.'

Ramaphosa underscored the conference's decision that land expropriation be 'among the mechanisms' used to give land back to its previous owners, but added the caveat that 'we must ensure that we do not undermine the economy, agricultural production and food security'. He was in favour of 'a radical path of socio-economic transformation, premised on growth, job creation and equitable distribution of income, wealth and assets'.

A large part of the speech was devoted to a pledge to 'act fearlessly against alleged corruption and abuse of office within our ranks'. 'Corruption', he said, 'must be fought with the same intensity and purpose that we fight poverty, unemployment and inequality.'

He finished with a tribute to Zuma, who appeared dazed at the swiftness with which he was losing his grip on power: 'I would like, on your behalf, to thank President Jacob Zuma for the ten years he has spent as the president of our movement and for a lifetime of service to the people of this country.'

Zuma had tasted defeat, but he wasn't done yet. He would fight one final battle to hold on to power.

# ELEVEN

# *Twelve days in February*

We should put all the negativity that has dogged our country
behind us because a new dawn is upon us.
*– Cyril Ramaphosa*

After the ANC conference ended a few days before Christmas, the
nation breathed a sigh of relief and politics gave way to the holidays. Ramaphosa's first step onto the world stage as ANC leader
would take place in January at the World Economic Forum in
Davos, the annual summit of the global business and political elite.
'They have been wanting to know if the process that we have now
started with of ridding our country of corruption is sustainable.
We've assured them that, yes, it is,'[1] he said in one of several television interviews.

Ramaphosa used the platform to reassure the investment community that state-owned enterprises would be placed on a sound
financial footing and that the government would deal with its fiscal
challenges responsibly. The message went down well with the
Davos audience and with South Africans, who finally saw a president calmly articulating a road to recovery.

But Ramaphosa was not yet president of the country.

Zuma's chosen successor might have been defeated in December, but Zuma remained president of the republic. Ramaphosa
had signalled that a new broom was sweeping out the dirt, yet

the man at the centre of the decade-long corruption scandal continued to occupy the highest office in the land.

With the 2019 election a year and a few months away, it was clear to all but the most die-hard Zuma supporter that, if Zuma had the party's interests at heart, he should step aside and allow Ramaphosa a shot at winning back the confidence of a sceptical electorate.

But Zuma was not going to go easily. The December conference had mandated the ANC's top six to manage the relationship between Zuma and Ramaphosa, and talks began over Zuma's departure. It soon became apparent that Zuma had no intention of leaving, at least not for several months. As January wore on, with Zuma still at the helm, Ramaphosa's patience was tested. Finally, in early February, the pressure on Zuma to quit was increased. What followed were 12 eventful days during which Zuma and the ANC performed a peculiar dance over his political future.

\*

On the first Sunday in February, the ANC's top six sent party deputy president David Mabuza to talk to Zuma about stepping down. Mabuza was apparently chosen in order to limit the awkwardness of a future president of the country negotiating his own accession to power. The meeting, at Zuma's official residence in Pretoria, went nowhere. Meanwhile, opposition parties began to call for a vote of no-confidence in Zuma to be debated in Parliament.

On the Monday after Mabuza's failed mission, the top six convened an emergency session of the party's NWC, which, in turn, called a meeting of the party's most powerful decision-making body, the NEC, for the following day. Having failed to persuade Zuma to do the right thing, the party's executive was now going to force him out by recalling him.

With the threat of a recall looming, Zuma became more cooper-

ative and held a meeting described as 'constructive' with Ramaphosa. Zuma had become a master at playing out processes to
defer decisions about his future. He had appealed every court
judgment against him all the way to the Constitutional Court, a
process that led to years of delay. Now he was playing for the
chance to serve out his full term as president of the country, and
Ramaphosa, for the moment, bought his story. To the annoyance
of some of his backers within the party, Ramaphosa called off the
Tuesday NEC meeting. He would make one final attempt to talk
Zuma down.

Zuma was scheduled to deliver the State of the Nation address
that Friday – a potentially embarrassing moment if the talks should
fail. This was remedied by getting Speaker of Parliament Baleka
Mbete to announce that the address had been postponed to some
unspecified point in the future.

Once the address had been postponed, the talks with Zuma
dragged on, though with little result. Finally, on Saturday 10 February, the top six met and decided to call a meeting of the party's
executive for Monday to make a final decision on his fate. The
meeting, at a hotel outside Pretoria, was the scene of late-night
drama. After several hours of discussion, a delegation was sent
to Zuma to make one final appeal. Zuma remained steadfast. The
delegation returned to the executive meeting and a decision was
taken to remove Zuma if he did not voluntarily step down by midnight on Wednesday.

The two factions that now lived uncomfortably side by side in
the ANC leadership were soon on public display. On Tuesday,
secretary general Ace Magashule was given the task of announcing
Zuma's recall at a media conference. His heart was not in it, to
the extent that he said, 'We did not take these decisions because
comrade Jacob Zuma has done anything wrong.'[2] His behaviour
was emblematic of the uncomfortable, inward-looking, defensive

politics of the Zuma era. In this world, the protection of the leader against the slings and arrows of criticism – and those flung by the criminal justice system – trumped all else. And so Magashule said, 'Forget about fake news [on] Russian nuclear or any other thing that disrespects President Zuma. We still believe in him as a leader.'[3]

Despite Zuma having done nothing wrong and the fact that he was still 'believed in' as a leader, Magashule said Zuma had been served with a letter explaining the party's decision to recall him. It was painful to watch.

There were several ways the party could remove Zuma. If he failed to heed the instruction to step down given by the executive, he could be voted out by a vote of no-confidence in Parliament. Finally, there was the possibility of removing him through impeachment, the consequence of which would be that he would lose all the benefits that usually accrue to a retired head of state. These benefits were substantial, and included funding for an office and its bureaucracy as well as access to travel and pay at the level of a head of state for life.

The opposition EFF had already tabled a motion of no-confidence in Zuma. On the same morning, the ANC parliamentary caucus resolved to table its own version of the motion. In stark contrast with Magashule, party treasurer Paul Mashatile did not mince his words in announcing the decision. Unless Zuma resigned by midnight on Tuesday, he would be voted out by a motion of no-confidence on Wednesday. Mashatile put it bluntly: 'Our people want to see change. They want to see the new leadership taking over the management, not only of the ANC but of the affairs of the state. We don't have time to be bickering about who should be president. We have elected president Ramaphosa, he should be the president. All is clear, that is how we move ahead.'[4]

As Mashatile spoke, television images of a series of police raids on Gupta homes and business premises were aired. The investigators struck at dawn, in search of evidence related to the Guptas' involvement in fleecing a dairy farm project in the Free State. Among those whose offices were raided was that of Magashule.

The nation waited for Zuma to respond to what was clearly a final demand that he step down or be fired.

On Wednesday, Zuma attempted one last act of political theatre, granting the SABC a televised interview, which was aired live. In an extraordinary performance that mixed self-pity with denial, Zuma mounted a rambling, shambolic defence of himself. Wearing a casual shirt and slumped in an armchair, repeatedly clearing his throat, Zuma said, 'I have not defied the party.'[5] He went on: 'When the top six came to see me . . . I asked . . . what was the problem? Why must I be persuaded to resign? Have I done anything wrong? Of course the officials couldn't provide what I have done . . . I need to be furnished [with] what I have done . . . I even asked: what is this hurry? What are you rushing for? . . . I'm not refusing to resign, it's a question of the timeframes.'[6]

Asked why he would not step down as graciously as his predecessor, Thabo Mbeki, had done, Zuma said, 'When the NEC discussed this matter, I am one of those who were in fact saying we should not recall comrade president Mbeki.'[7] It was a statement that contradicted the well-known fact that Zuma had insisted that Mbeki leave office before his term as president was up. Zuma appeared to have lost touch with reality.

Perhaps Zuma believed that, once he had put his point of view across on television, the ANC leadership would relent. But the reverse happened. The interview was evidence even to his most diehard supporters, that he had to go.

That evening, Zuma resigned in a nationally televised address at the Union Buildings. It was another off-key performance. Zuma appeared defiant and defensive. He raised the question of his perks and benefits: 'There has been much speculation about how the

President of the Republic should exit his or her office. In my case, some have even dared to suggest that one's perks and post-service benefits should determine how one chooses to vacate public office. Often these concerns about perks and benefits are raised by the very same people seeking to speak as paragons of virtue and all things constitutional.'[8]

Eventually, he announced: 'I have therefore come to the decision to resign as President of the Republic with immediate effect.'[9] Zuma's resignation was submitted to the Speaker and his decade of misrule finally came to a grinding halt.

*

The next day, Ramaphosa was sworn in as president by Chief Justice Mogoeng Mogoeng, as the nation recovered from its cele-bration of the end of the Zuma era. Ramaphosa, wearing a grey suit and red tie, had finally arrived at the crowning moment of his political career. His family and supporters from the benches of Parliament gathered to witness the event at Tuynhuys, the office of the president adjacent to Parliament in Cape Town.

Mogoeng said, 'It is a great honour and privilege to invite our president-elect of the Republic of South Africa, to take an oath or affirmation . . . Your excellency, is it going to be an oath or an affirmation?'

'Oath,' replied Ramaphosa.

Ramaphosa repeated after Mogoeng: 'In the presence of every-one assembled here, and in full realisation of the high calling I assume, as president of the Republic of South Africa, I, Matamela Cyril Ramaphosa, swear that I will be faithful to the Republic of South Africa and will obey, observe, uphold and main-tain the Constitution and all other law of the republic.

'I solemnly and sincerely promise that I will always promote all that will advance the republic and oppose all that may harm it, protect and promote the rights of all South Africans, discharge my duties with all my strength and talents to the best of my knowledge and ability and true to the dictates of my conscience, do justice to all and devote myself to the wellbeing of the republic and all of its people.'

Ramaphosa raised his right hand and swore: 'So help me God.'[10]

\*

After months of prevarication, everything suddenly seemed to be moving at breakneck speed. The following evening, Ramaphosa rose in Parliament to deliver his first State of the Nation address. In his opening remarks, he mentioned his predecessor: 'I also wish to extend a word of gratitude to former President Jacob Zuma for the manner in which he approached this difficult and sensitive process.'[11] Zuma, still nursing his wounds, was pointedly absent from the House.

Ramaphosa began with a commitment to serving the spirit of Nelson Mandela: 'We have dedicated this year to his memory and we will devote our every action, every effort, every utterance to the realisation of his vision of a democratic, just and equitable society.' The soundbite that would be echoed for weeks to come was uttered as Ramaphosa said, 'We should put all the negativity that has dogged our country behind us because a new dawn is upon us . . . There are 57 million of us, each with different histories, languages, cultures, experiences, views and interests. Yet we are bound together by a common destiny.'

It was a speech that came down hard on corruption, pledged a change in the way the nation did business and promised transformation to the excluded and unemployed youth. Ramaphosa played to his strength as a negotiator, promising a series of meetings, commissions and consultations aimed at getting government, business and labour to find common ground.

The land question was addressed: 'We will accelerate our land redistribution programme not only to redress a grave historical injustice, but also to bring more producers into the agricultural sector and to make more land available for cultivation. We will pursue a comprehensive approach that makes effective use of all the mechanisms at our disposal. Guided by the resolutions of the 54th National Conference of the governing party, this approach will include the expropriation of land without compensation.'

Zuma's last-minute intervention before the December conference, when he announced free higher education, also found its way into the speech.

The consensus was that Ramaphosa had introduced a new sense of optimism. The rand strengthened as commentators began to talk positively about the possibility of economic growth for the first time in years.

But the euphoria would soon be dimmed by the relentless grind of politics.

Barely two weeks after Ramaphosa took office, the ANC took the momentous decision to vote in favour of an EFF motion that a committee investigate a constitutional amendment to allow for the expropriation of farmland without compensation. Speaking in the debate, Gugile Nkwinti, the former Land Reform minister, said, 'The ANC unequivocally supports the principle of land expropriation without compensation. There is no doubt about it, land shall be expropriated without compensation.'[12]

*

On 26 February, Ramaphosa announced a new Cabinet. He had promised that things would run on time, but the Cabinet announcement was delayed for an hour and half as he appeared to be making final consultations. When he finally announced the Cabinet, observers said he seemed grim, perhaps even a little defeated.[13]

He had promised to reduce the size of the executive, but this would only take place once an investigation had been completed. For now, Ramaphosa reshuffled Zuma's Cabinet. There were refreshing changes, such as the return of Nhlanhla Nene – fired by Zuma – to the position of Finance minister, and the appointment of Pravin Gordhan to the Public Enterprises portfolio. The message was clear: Zuma's plan to turn the Treasury and state-owned companies into a money-making machine for his cronies was dead and buried.

But Ramaphosa's precarious hold on power was also showing. David Mabuza – the man who had engineered his victory at the party conference in December – would be his deputy president. The controversial Mpumalanga power broker, who had been linked to several serious scandals, was now a heartbeat away from the presidency.

Ramaphosa fired several Zuma loyalists, such as the Mineral Resources minister, Mosebenzi Zwane, and Des van Rooyen, whom Zuma had attempted unsuccessfully to install as Finance minister, but he retained others. The hapless Bathabile Dlamini, who had failed to sort out the mess around social grants, was given a portfolio in the Presidency along with Nkosazana Dlamini-Zuma, whom Ramaphosa had defeated. And Malusi Gigaba was returned to the Home Affairs ministry where he had overseen the naturalisation of the Guptas, paving the way for them to conclude the swathe of business deals around state capture. Bheki Cele, the disgraced former national police commissioner who had signed off on dodgy leases, returned as Police minister.

After a start that had promised so much, Ramaphosa appeared to have been dragged into the political maw. He had fulfilled his ambition to scale the heights of political power. But now he would have to summon all of his patience, negotiating skill and political nous to turn his presidency into a new beginning for the nation.

# Postscript

Everyone wants to know what South Africa's new president, Cyril Ramaphosa, is all about. What does he stand for? What are his politics? How does he operate?

The first two questions are easily answered.

To understand what Ramaphosa stands for, look no further than the Constitution, which bears his imprint. As the ANC's chief negotiator, he played a larger role than anyone else in its formulation. It is a document with a strong Bill of Rights protecting individual freedom. But it is also a social charter, setting all future governments on a course to address social injustice and to prevent the birth of new injustices. It creates a modern democratic state with a high degree of accountability. But it also directs the state to be compassionate and to place the marginalised, the poor and the discriminated against at the centre of its programmes.

These are Ramaphosa's foundational values. Nelson Mandela is his lodestar. In his first State of the Nation address, Ramaphosa spoke of 'a new dawn that is inspired by our collective memory of Nelson Mandela'.[1]

Ramaphosa's politics are also easy to discern. He is a pragmatic social democrat who enjoys the support of the ANC's left and the respect of those parts of business that embrace democratic South Africa. The trade union federation Cosatu was the first institution to publicly back his campaign for the presidency.

He is not one to approach problems from an ideological perspective. He has spent time at the highest levels of both the trade union movement and business, and is uniquely placed to view problems of growth and investment through both these prisms.

It is the third question – 'How does he operate?' – that is the most difficult and, therefore, the most intriguing. There is an easy answer, which has been given many times – that Ramaphosa is a negotiator.

The State of the Nation address was essentially a commitment to lead South Africa out of its mess by negotiation. He promised a number of new initiatives: a jobs summit 'to align the efforts of every sector and every stakeholder behind the imperative of job creation', an investment conference, 'to market the compelling investment opportunities to be found in our country'; a promise to 'engage stakeholders' over the contentious mining charter; a digital industrial revolution commission, 'which will include the private sector and civil society'; a presidential economic advisory council, which would draw 'on the expertise and capabilities that reside in labour, business, civil society and academia'; and the implementation of a minimum wage, which he negotiated at Nedlac while deputy president, 'made possible by the determination of all social partners'.[2]

There is no doubt that Ramaphosa is comfortable when he is sitting at a table to debate and discuss solutions. It is his terrain, one where he wins. Negotiating the transition from apartheid to democracy was no walk in the park, whatever the twitterati might say.

But this is not the whole answer. Like magicians, politicians never give a full account of their tricks, but a lot can be told from observing at a distance. Ramaphosa's real talent lies in playing the long game. When he left politics in 1996, his ambition to succeed Mandela thwarted by the ANC's exile lobby, he became a businessman, but he always had a return to politics in mind. Patience is a key pillar of the long game.

Sixteen years later, in 2012, as Zuma foundered and the ANC began to lose its grip on public support, the opportunity opened up and he returned to take up the position of deputy president. From then on, the long game had one simple objective: amassing a majority of the votes of the 5000-odd delegates at the ANC's 2017 elective conference.

The rules of the long game dictate that the goal – however distant, however apparently unattainable, however wrapped in the mists of future politics – is the only thing that matters. Actions fall into two categories: those that help you attain your goal and those that hinder it. The game is made more complicated by the ANC's internal culture, which dictates that criticism should be kept behind closed doors and unity shown to the public.

And so the long game dictated that Ramaphosa had to grin and bear it at Zuma's side as scandals erupted. Sometimes he appeared complicit and sometimes inexplicably silent. The long game dictates that your opponent must be kept comfortably numb, oblivious to your encroachment until it is too late. When you strike, victory must be certain.

And so Ramaphosa stayed loyal to Zuma in public, all the while drawing into his camp the disaffected – premiers fired without good reason, provinces losing voter support because of corruption, veterans afraid their legacy was being destroyed, Cabinet ministers relieved of their duties because they clashed with Zuma over state capture.

When the moment was right – in mid-2017 – Ramaphosa had sufficient traction within the party, and he struck, calling for those behind state capture to be tried and jailed, and for the money they had taken to be paid back. But even then, although the inference was clear, he did not directly attack Zuma. Ramaphosa was fighting a master of the political arts, a man who had outwitted Thabo Mbeki and mounted one of the greatest comebacks in modern politics.

The best way to understand how Ramaphosa outplayed Zuma is by analogy, and, so, a brief digression.

The Second World War film *Thunderbolt* is a rousing work of propaganda that generously credits the American P-47 Thunderbolt fighter-bomber for the Allied victory in northern Italy. Like all war 'documentaries', this one has to be taken with a pinch of salt. The reality was no doubt not nearly as simple. But the story nonetheless contains a metaphor for the politics of the long game.

The film recounts how Allied forces invaded Sicily and then stormed up the Italian peninsula before being stopped in their tracks by stubborn German resistance in the Apennine Mountains of central Italy. It was a deadly stalemate with a high body count.

A new strategy was developed. The Thunderbolts were launched from airfields in Corsica with the purpose of systematically destroying the German lines of supply across northern Italy. They bombed and strafed road and rail infrastructure, erasing bridges and destroying trains on the tracks. All of this, quite remarkably for the time, was captured on film by cameras mounted on the wings and cockpits of the planes.

The result of the air campaign was a dramatic reduction in fuel, food and ammunition supplies to the Germans entrenched in the Apennines. When the time was right, the Allies advanced through the mountains, crushing a much-reduced enemy who was worn out, hungry and short of fuel.

The role of the Thunderbolt in the Italian campaign is probably exaggerated, but here's the important point it makes: there is little to be gained but attrition when you directly confront a powerful enemy in terrain that favours them. The right approach is to isolate them, strangle them, take away their resources and then, when the playing field tilts decisively in your favour, turn up the pressure until they capitulate.

This digression into the Italian campaign is the best way I can think of to describe how Ramaphosa unseated Zuma once he had defeated Zuma's candidate of choice, Nkosazana Dlamini-Zuma, at the ANC's December 2017 conference. Ramaphosa won, but by a narrow majority. The long game now had a new objective: the removal of Zuma and the grand prize of the presidency of the country. Instead of a direct war of attrition with a high body count, Ramaphosa mobilised his Thunderbolts to cut off Zuma's lines of supply.

The most dramatic gesture was the replacement of the Eskom board with credible, competent and respected leaders, with Jabu Mabuza as the new chairman. The giant state-owned enterprise sat at the centre of Zuma's spider's web of state capture. It had been converted into a funnel through which state bail-out money flowed to the Guptas and captured board members through multi-billion-rand coal contracts, inflated salaries and golden handshakes.

By snatching Eskom rudely out of Zuma's hands, Ramaphosa sent a clear message that the old order was dying, its lines of supply cut off. Zuma no longer had patronage to dispense. To the middle ground in the ANC leadership, the message was clear: it was time to shuffle sheepishly in the direction of the Ramaphosa camp.

There were more Thunderbolts. Ramaphosa made it plain that he expected the prosecution service and the Hawks to act decisively against corruption. NPA head Shaun 'The Sheep' Abrahams, who had protected Zuma's empire by omitting to act, now zipped on wolf's clothing. Case files were dusted off. Dairy farms, Eskom headquarters and – ten years too late – the Gupta compound were raided by policemen in bulletproof vests.

The momentum having shifted decisively, it was finally time to act. Even then, Ramaphosa declined to confront. His impatient supporters were surprised when he unilaterally postponed an NEC meeting to oust Zuma in favour of one more round of talks. By not confronting Zuma, Ramaphosa removed his final weapon: his ability to play the victim, to call on his supporters to fight for his dignity.

When the NEC eventually met, not one member spoke up for Zuma staying in office. In the ultimate symbol of capitulation, one of Zuma's most loyal supporters, the Water and Sanitation minister Nomvula Mokonyane, is said to have declined to speak at all, claiming to have the flu.

Zuma was out, and, within days, Ramaphosa was delivering the State of the Nation address to a standing ovation from the House. After that, there was one final move in the long game: a farewell dinner for a defeated and bewildered enemy, filled with the laughter of the victor.

# Acknowledgements

I owe Jeremy Boraine a debt of gratitude for inspiring me to write this book and providing me with the support and encouragement I needed when I was flagging. Jeremy's good humour and his steely insistence that I would make it to the end pushed me over the finish line.

And I must once more thank Alfred LeMaitre for applying his incisive editing mind to the manuscript. His perceptive remarks, suggestions and questions made this a far better book than it would have been without his eye.

This book would not have been possible without the writing of South Africa's many excellent journalists and commentators, who have, between them, placed this country's unfolding drama on record. Anthony Butler's *Cyril Ramaphosa* is a delight to read, and this book leans heavily on its insights and research to flesh out the life of Ramaphosa. Also indispensable was Mark Gevisser's biography of Thabo Mbeki, *The Dream Deferred*, which remains one of the best works of political biography written about a South African. Because of the entanglement between the political ambitions of Mbeki and Ramaphosa, Gevisser's book was an essential resource.

I made use of numerous other biographies, histories and autobiographies for this book. A select bibliography can be found on the page that follows this. Other sources are listed in the notes.

I would also like to thank all those who agreed to speak to me on and off the record.

I owe my wife, Sylvia, and my daughter, Zoë, thanks for their patience as I once more turned the house into a sprawling, untidy research station. I dedicated my first book, *Ragged Glory: The Rainbow Nation in Black and White*, to my father, Thomas Hartley, 'who inspired me to read and to think'. He passed away as I was finishing the writing of this book and I would like to acknowledge him once more. I persevered with writing even as my days were clouded in grief. He won't be around to offer me his observations and I am the poorer for it.

# Select bibliography

Asmal, Kader and Adrian Hadland, with Moira Levy. *Kader Asmal: Politics in my Blood – A Memoir* (Jacana, 2011).

Barnard, Niël. *Secret Revolution: Memoirs of a Spy Boss* (Tafelberg, 2015).

Barnard, Niël, with Tobie Wiese. *Peaceful Revolution: Inside the War Room at the Negotiations* (Tafelberg, 2017).

Butler, Anthony. *Cyril Ramaphosa* (Jacana, 2007).

Calland, Richard. *The Zuma Years: South Africa's Changing Face of Power* (Zebra Press, 2013).

Copelyn, Johnny. *Maverick Insider: A Struggle for Union Independence in a Time of National Liberation* (Picador Africa, 2016).

De Klerk, FW. *The Last Trek – A New Beginning. The Autobiography* (St Martin's Press, 1998).

Forrest, Kally. *Metal That Will Not Bend: The National Union of Metalworkers of South Africa, 1980–1995* (Wits University Press, 2011).

Gevisser, Mark. *Thabo Mbeki: The Dream Deferred* (Jonathan Ball, 2007).

Gumede, William Mervyn. *Thabo Mbeki and the Battle for the Soul of the ANC* (Zebra Press, 2007).

Hadland, Adrian and Jovial Rantao. *The Life and Times of Thabo Mbeki* (Zebra Press, 1999).

Harvey, Ebrahim. *Kgalema Motlanthe: A Political Biography* (Jacana, 2012).

Jeffery, Anthea. *BEE: Helping or Hurting?* (Tafelberg, 2014).

Lodge, Tom. *Black Politics in South Africa since 1945* (Ravan Press, 1983).

Mandela, Nelson. *Long Walk to Freedom* (Macdonald Purnell, 1994).

———. *In His Own Words: From Freedom to the Future*. Edited by Kader Asmal, David Chidester and Wilmot James (Abacus, 2003).

Marinovich, Greg. *Murder at Small Koppie: The Real Story of the Marikana Massacre* (Penguin, 2016).

Moseneke, Dikgang. *My Own Liberator: A Memoir* (Picador Africa, 2016).

Myburgh, Pieter-Louis. *The Republic of Gupta: The Story of State Capture* (Penguin, 2017).

Naidoo, Jay. *Fighting for Justice: A Lifetime of Political and Social Activism* (Picador Africa, 2010).

O'Malley, Padraig. *Shades of Difference: Mac Maharaj and the Struggle for South Africa* (Penguin, 2008).

Simpson, Thula. *Umkhonto we Sizwe: The ANC's Armed Struggle* (Penguin, 2016).

Slovo, Joe. *Slovo: The Unfinished Autobiography of ANC Leader Joe Slovo* (Ravan, 1995).

Waldmeir, Patti. *Anatomy of a Miracle: The End of Apartheid and the Birth of the New South Africa* (Viking, 1997).

# Notes

## Introduction

1    Anthony Butler, *Cyril Ramaphosa* (Jacana, 2007), Preface, p x.

2    News24, 'Zuma like a "tsunami wave"', 7 March 2005. Available at www.news24.com/SouthAfrica/News/Zuma-like-a-"tsunami-wave" -20050307, accessed on 2 October 2017.

3    Goldman Sachs, 'Two Decades of Freedom', report, 4 November 2013. Available at www.goldmansachs.com/our-thinking/archive/colin-coleman-south-africa/20-yrs-of-freedom.pdf, accessed on 2 October 2017.

## Chapter 1: Consciousness

1    Anthony Butler, *Cyril Ramaphosa* (Jacana, 2007), p 30.

2    Barney Pityana, 'In Memory of Bantu Stephen Biko – A Personal Testimony', 9 September 2017. Available at www.mbeki.org/2017/09/11/in-memory-of-bantu-stephen-biko-a-personal-testimony/, accessed on 2 October 2017.

3    Bantu Stephen Biko, 'The Definition of Black Consciousness', essay, December 1971.

4    Ibid.

5    Butler, *Cyril Ramaphosa*, p 45.

6    Ibid, p 51.

7    Frances Baard and Barbie Schreiner, *My Spirit is Not Banned*, online book, 1986. Available at www.sahistory.org.za/archive/my-spirit-not-banned, accessed on 6 September 2017.

8    Ibid.

9    'Black Consciousness Movement', South African History Online. Available at www.sahistory.org.za/article/bikos-imprisonment-death-and-aftermath, accessed on 6 September 2017.

10   Butler, *Cyril Ramaphosa*, p 64.

11   Ibid, p 68.

12   Ibid, p 14.

13   Truth and Reconciliation Commission, Human Rights Violations Submissions – Questions and Answers, 4 October 1996, Simon Farisani, Day 2. Available at www.justice.gov.za/trc/hrvtrans%5Cvenda/farisani.htm, accessed on 6 September 2017.

14 Ibid.

15 Butler, *Cyril Ramaphosa*, p 32.

16 'National Congress Address by National President, Mr T. S. Farisani', 1975, p 1. Available at disa.ukzn.ac.za/sites/default/files/pdf_files/ spe19751213.032.009.286.pdf, accessed on 6 September 2017.

17 Tom Lodge, *Black Politics in South Africa since 1945* (Ravan Press, 1983), p 34.

18 Ibid, p 339.

19 Ibid, p 340.

## Chapter 2: **The man who sat across the table**

1 'Cyril Matamela Ramaphosa', SA History Online, 5 July 2017. Available at www.sahistory.org.za/people/cyril-matamela-ramaphosa, accessed on 2 October 2017.

2 Kally Forrest, *Metal That Will Not Bend: The National Union of Metalworkers of South Africa, 1980–1995* (Wits University Press, 2011), p 109.

3 Anthony Butler, *Cyril Ramaphosa* (Jacana, 2007), p 137.

4 Ibid, p 156.

5 'Congress of South African Trade Unions (COSATU)', South African History Online, 1 December 2016. Available at www.sahistory.org.za/topic/ congress-south-african-trade-unions-cosatu, accessed on 6 September 2017.

6 Jay Naidoo, *Fighting for Justice: A Lifetime of Political and Social Activism* (Picador Africa, 2010), p 97.

7 Johnny Copelyn, *Maverick Insider: A Struggle for Union Independence in a Time of National Liberation* (Picador Africa, 2016), p 249.

8 Naidoo, *Fighting for Justice*, p 98.

9 Ibid, p 8.

10 Joe Slovo, *Slovo: The Unfinished Autobiography of ANC Leader Joe Slovo* (Ravan, 1995), p 222.

11 Ibid.

12 Ibid.

13 Padraig O'Malley, *Shades of Difference: Mac Maharaj and the Struggle for South Africa* (Penguin, 2008), p 281.

14 Ebrahim Harvey, *Kgalema Motlanthe: A Political Biography* (Jacana, 2012), p 77.

15 Ibid.

16 Naidoo, *Fighting for Justice*.

17 Anton Harber, 'Ramaphosa made history confronting Oppenheimer',

*Business Day*, 30 August 2017. Available at www.businesslive.co.za/bd/opinion/2017-08-30-anton-harber-ramaphosa-made-history-confronting-oppenheimer/, accessed on 7 September 2017.

18  Ibid.
19  Ibid.
20  Ibid.
21  Jade Davenport, 'The 1987 mine strike', *Mining Weekly*, 27 September 2013.
22  This and subsequent quotations, as well as descriptions of the events that followed, unless otherwise attributed, are from *History Uncut*, video documentaries, Afravision.
23  *Weekly Mail*, 10 January 1987.
24  Davenport, 'The 1987 mine strike'.
25  Author's interview with Bobby Godsell.
26  Naidoo, *Fighting for Justice*, p 139.
27  Davenport, 'The 1987 mine strike'.
28  TK Philip, 'NUM, the 1987 strike and its aftermath: a social history', no date. Available at wiredspace.wits.ac.za, accessed on 7 September 2017.
29  *History Uncut*.
30  Copelyn, *Maverick Insider*, p 214.
31  *History Uncut*.
32  Ibid.
33  John Battersby, 'Miners end strike in South Africa with no wage gain', *The New York Times*, 31 August 1987.
34  Ibid.
35  Ibid.

## Chapter 3: **Mandela's chosen one**

1  Nelson Mandela, *Long Walk to Freedom* (Macdonald Purnell, 1994), p 543.
2  Ibid, p 551.
3  Jay Naidoo, *Fighting for Justice: A Lifetime of Political and Social Activism* (Picador Africa, 2010), p 6.
4  'Mandela's speech from the City Hall steps', archived transcript, *Mail & Guardian*. Available at mg.co.za/article/1990-02-12-mandelas-speech-from-the-city-hall-steps, accessed on 2 October 2017.
5  Mark Gevisser, *Thabo Mbeki: The Dream Deferred* (Jonathan Ball, 2007), p 570.
6  Mandela, *Long Walk to Freedom*, p 583.
7  Gevisser, *Thabo Mbeki*, p 602.
8  Ibid, p 604.

9    Padraig O'Malley interview with Ramaphosa, 16 August 1991. Available at
     www.nelsonmandela.org/omalley/index.php/site/q/03lv00017/
     04lv00344/05lv00511/06lv00560.htm, accessed on 8 September 2017.
10   William Mervyn Gumede, *Thabo Mbeki and the Battle for the Soul of the
     ANC* (Zebra, 2007), p 34.
11   Ibid.
12   Nelson Mandela, *In His Own Words: From Freedom to the Future*, edited
     by Kader Asmal, David Chidester and Wilmot James (Abacus, 2003), pp
     145–146.
13   Richard Calland, *The Zuma Years: South Africa's Changing Face of Power*
     (Zebra Press, 2013), pp 167–168.
14   Kader Asmal and Adrian Hadland, with Moira Levy, *Kader Asmal: Politics
     in my Blood – A Memoir* (Jacana, 2011), p 206.
15   Naidoo, *Fighting for Justice*, p 176.

## Chapter 4: **The big deal**

1    Padraig O'Malley interview with Cyril Ramaphosa, 16 August 1991. Avail-
     able at www.nelsonmandela.org/omalley/index.php/site/q/03lv00017/
     04lv00344/05lv00511/06lv00560.htm, accessed on 8 September 2017.
2    Ibid.
3    Niël Barnard with Tobie Wiese, *Peaceful Revolution: Inside the War Room
     at the Negotiations* (Tafelberg, 2017), p 29.
4    Ibid, pp 29–30.
5    Ibid, p 30.
6    Padraig O'Malley interview with Ramaphosa, 16 August 1991.
7    Hilton Tarrant, 'Who is Cyril Ramaphosa? Roelf Meyer – former Minister
     of Constitutional Affairs and Minister of Constitutional Development',
     Moneyweb, 19 December 2012. Available at www.moneyweb.co.za/
     archive/r-526/, accessed on 12 September 2017
8    Ibid.
9    David Honigmann, 'The Roelf 'n' Cyril show', *Independent*, 10 June 1995.
10   Tarrant, 'Who is Cyril Ramaphosa?'.
11   Lesley Cowling, 'How Cyril lands the big fish', *Mail & Guardian*, 26 May
     1995.
12   Ibid.
13   'Interview: Roelf Meyer', Helen Suzman Foundation, 2 October 2009.
     Available at hsf.org.za/resource-centre/focus/issue-14-second-quarter-
     1999/interview-roelf-meyer, accessed on 12 September 2017.
14   Ibid.

15  Thula Simpson, *Umkhonto we Sizwe: the ANC's Armed Struggle* (Penguin, 2016), p 489.
16  Ibid.
17  Ibid, p 490.
18  Melanie Verwoerd, 'Roelf Meyer: "We had bigger challenges then than we do now"', Daily Maverick, 30 June 2016. Available at www.dailymaverick. co.za/article/2016-06-30-we-had-bigger-challenges-then-than-we-do-now-roelf-meyer, accessed on 12 September 2017.
19  Ibid.
20  'Meyer recalls role in SA's democratic transition', University of Cape Town News, 30 April 2014. Available at www.news.uct.ac.za/article/-2014-04-30-meyer-recalls-role-in-sas-democratic-transition, accessed on 12 September 2017.
21  Ibid.
22  Padraig O'Malley, *Shades of Difference: Mac Maharaj and the Struggle for South Africa* (Penguin, 2008), p 392.
23  Patti Waldmeir, *Anatomy of a Miracle: The End of Apartheid and the Birth of the New South Africa* (Viking, 1997), p 210.
24  Ibid, p 211.
25  FW de Klerk, *The Last Trek – A New Beginning. The Autobiography* (St Martin's Press, 1998), p 210.
26  Padraig O'Malley interview with Roelf Meyer, 13 August 1993. Available at www.nelsonmandela.org/omalley/index.php/site/q/03lv00017/04lv00344/05lv00730/06lv00769.htm, accessed on 12 September 2017.
27  Joe Slovo, *Slovo: The Unfinished Autobiography of ANC Leader Joe Slovo* (Ravan, 1995), p 223.
28  O'Malley, *Shades of Difference*, p 402.
29  Constitution of the Republic of South Africa Act 200 of 1993, preamble. Available at www.gov.za/documents/constitution/constitution-republic-south-africa-act-200-1993, accessed on 12 September 2017.
30  Ibid, section 8(2).
31  Ibid, section 28(1).
32  Mark Gevisser, *Thabo Mbeki: The Dream Deferred* (Jonathan Ball, 2007), p 623.
33  Ibid.
34  'South African general election, 2104', Wikipedia, 29 July 2017. Available at en.wikipedia.org/wiki/South_African_general_election,_2014, accessed on 12 September 2017.
35  'Secretary General's Report to ANC 49th National Conference'. Available

at www.anc.org.za/content/49th-national-conference-secretary-generals-report, accessed on 12 September 2017.

## Chapter 5: **The commanding heights of business**

1   Johnnies Industrial Corporation, or Johnnic, was formed when Anglo American split its subsidiary, Johannesburg Consolidated Investment Company (JCI), into three separate companies.

2   Mark Gevisser, *Thabo Mbeki: The Dream Deferred* (Jonathan Ball, 2007), p 587.

3   'Nthato Harrison Motlana', South African History Online, 26 October 2011. Available at www.sahistory.org.za/people/nthato-harrison-motlana, accessed on 12 September 2017.

4   Dikgang Moseneke, *My Own Liberator: A Memoir* (Picador Africa, 2017), p 329.

5   Ibid.

6   Author's interview with Cyril Ramaphosa. All quotations from Cyril Ramaphosa in this chapter are from the author's interview with him, unless otherwise stated.

7   Author's interview with Michael Spicer. All quotations from Michael Spicer in this chapter are from the author's interview with him, unless otherwise stated.

8   Thebe Mabanga, 'Clash of the titans', *Mail & Guardian*, 8 July 2005. Available at mg.co.za/article/2005-07-08-clash-of-the-titans, accessed on 12 September 2017.

9   Ibid.

10  Ronnie Morris, 'R244m for HCI as Johnnic announces R500m payout', *Business Report*, 19 January 2006. Available at www.iol.co.za/business-report/economy/r244m-for-hci-as-johnnic-announces-r500m-payout-743179, accessed on 12 September 2017.

11  Ibid.

12  Rob Rose, 'Calling the shots', *Financial Mail*, republished by HCI, 18 January 2012. Available at www.hci.co.za/general/calling-the-shots/, accessed on 12 September 2017.

13  Anthony Butler, *Cyril Ramaphosa* (Jacana, 2007), p 340.

14  Moseneke, *My Own Liberator*, p 33.

15  Anthea Jeffery, *BEE: Helping or Hurting?* (Tafelberg, 2014), p 137.

16  'Company overview', Shanduka section of Phembani website, 2016. Available at www.phembani.com/index.php/history-of-shanduka/, accessed on 12 September 2017.

17   Ibid.

18   Mmanaledi Mataboge, 'Ramaphosa withdraws from Shanduka Group', *Mail & Guardian*, 27 May 2014.

19   Ibid.

20   Sapa, 'Zuma approves extension for Ramaphosa', 16 August 2014

21   Trust Matsilele, 'Ramaphosa breaks away from Shanduka', CNBC Africa, 26 November 2014.

22   Pieter-Louis Myburgh, *The Republic of Gupta: A Story of State Capture* (Penguin, 2017), p 168.

23   Ibid.

24   Ibid, p 169.

25   Ibid.

26   Ibid, p 170.

27   Ibid.

28   Ibid, p 171.

29   Ibid.

30   Ibid.

31   Sam Sole and Susan Comrie, 'How Brian Molefe "helped" Gupta Optimum heist', amabhungane.co.za, 16 May 2017. Available at amabhungane.co.za/article/2017-05-16-exclusive-how-brian-molefe-helped-gupta-optimum-heist, accessed on 13 September 2017.

32   Ibid.

33   Ibid.

34   Myburgh, *The Republic of Gupta*, p 172.

35   Ibid.

36   Charlotte Mathews, 'Mining: minister's Gupta trip', Financial Mail, 28 January 2016. Available at www.businesslive.co.za/fm/fm-fox/2016-01-28-mining-ministers-gupta-trip/, accessed on 13 September 2017.

37   Jeffery, *BEE*, p 159.

38   Phakamisa Ndzamela, 'Black investment groups' strategies evolve', *Business Day*, 29 April 2015. Available at www.businesslive.co.za/bd/companies/financial-services/2015-04-29-black-investment-groups-strategies-evolve/, accessed on 13 September 2017.

39   Parliament of the Republic of South Africa, Joint Committee on Ethics and Members' Interests, 'Register of Members' Interests, 2016'. Available at www.parliament.gov.za/storage/app/media/PRandNews/content/Parliament_of_RSA_2016_Register.pdf, accessed on 13 September 2017.

40   'Buffalo soldier Cyril loses out', *City Press*, 14 April 2012. Available at city-press.news24.com/SouthAfrica/News/Buffalo-soldier-Cyril-loses-out-20120414, accessed on 13 September 2017.

41    Julius Malema, 'The hypocrisy of Cyril Ramaphosa – Julius Malema', Letter from the Commander in Chief, EFF, Politicsweb, 13 November 2013. Available at www.politicsweb.co.za/news-and-analysis/the-hypocrisy-of-cyril-ramaphosa--julius-malema, accessed on 13 September 2017.

42    'Ramaphosa sorry about "R18m" buffalo', *City Press*, 20 September 2012.

43    Adriaan Kruger, 'Johann Rupert pays R40m for buffalo bull', Fin24, 20 September 2013. Available at www.fin24.com/Economy/Johann-Rupert-pays-R45m-for-buffalo-bull-20130920, accessed on 13 September 2017.

44    Sean Christie, 'Speaking to Cyril Ramaphosa about game breeding', *Farmer's Weekly*, 22 May 2012. Available at www.farmersweekly.co.za/bottomline/speaking-to-cyril-ramaphosa-about-game-breeding/, accessed on 13 September 2017.

45    Ibid.

46    Ibid.

47    Gerhard Uys, 'Cyril Ramaphosa's Ankole bull sells for R640 000', *Farmer's Weekly*, 12 May 2017. Available at www.farmersweekly.co.za/agri-news/south-africa/cyril-ramaphosas-ankole-bull-sells-r640-000/, accessed on 13 September 2017.

## Chapter 6: The depths of Marikana

1    Greg Marinovich, *Murder at Small Koppie: The Real Story of the Marikana Massacre* (Penguin, 2016), p 136.

2    'The Marikana Commission of Inquiry: Report on matters of public, national and international concern arising out of the tragic incidents at the London mine Marikana, in the North West Province', 31 March 2015. Unless otherwise indicated, all quotations referring to 'the commission' in this chapter are taken from the report.

3    Martin Creamer, 'Emerging Amcu mine union favours competitive co-existence', *Mining Weekly*, 6 June 2012. Available at www.miningweekly.com/article/emerging-amcu-mine-union-favours-competitive-coexistence-joseph-mathunjwa-2012-06-06, accessed on 2 October 2017.

4    Bongani Madondo, '"We can't watch as the country sinks", says Ramaphosa', *Sunday Times*, 25 June 2017. Available at www.timeslive.co.za/sunday-times/news/2017-06-24-we-cant-watch-as-the-country-sinks-says-ramaphosa/, accessed on 13 September 2017.

5    TimesLive, 'Union leader Mathunjwa rejects Ramaphosa apology', TimesLive, 9 May 2017. Available at www.dispatchlive.co.za/politics/2017/05/09/union-leader-mathunjwa-rejects-ramaphosa-apology/, accessed on 13 September 2017.

6    Marinovich, *Murder at Small Koppie*, p 139.
7    Ibid.

## Chapter 7: **Return to politics**

1    Once the constitutional negotiations had been completed, both Rama-phosa and Roelf Meyer were asked to help find ways of negotiating politi-cal solutions to intractable problems in places such as Northern Ireland.
2    Chris McGreal, 'ANC veterans accused of plot to harm Mbeki', *The Guardian*, 26 April 2001. Available at www.theguardian.com/world/2001/apr/26/chrismcgreal, accessed on 13 October 2017.
3    Author's interview with Cyril Ramaphosa.
4    Baldwin Ndaba and Gcina Ntsaluba, 'Stop Malema now, says Cyril', IOL, 18 April 2012. Available at www.iol.co.za/pretoria-news/stop-malema-now-says-cyril-1279006, accessed on 14 September 2017.
5    Ranjeni Munusamy, 'Cyril Ramaphosa: the return of Nelson Mandela's chosen one', Daily Maverick and Guardian Africa Network, 20 Decem-ber 2012.
6    Deshnee Subramany, 'Mangaung: The ANC's newly elected top six', *Mail & Guardian*, 18 December 2012.
7    Amogelang Mbatha, 'Ramaphosa set to be SA's deputy president', Money-web, 16 May 2014. Available at www.moneyweb.co.za/archive/ramaphosa-set-to-be-sas-deputy-president/, accessed on 15 September 2017.
8    Ibid.

## Chapter 8: **Crisis point**

1    Mandy Rossouw, 'Zuma's R65m Nkandla splurge', *Mail & Guardian*, 4 December 2009. Available at mg.co.za/article/2009-12-04-zumas-r65m-nkandla-splurge, accessed on 16 October 2017.
2    Sapa, 'Madonsela accused of being a CIA spy', *Mail & Guardian*, 8 Septem-ber 2014. Available at mg.co.za/article/2014-09-08-madonsela-accused-of-being-a-cia-spy, accessed on 2 October 2017.
3    Public Protector South Africa, 'Secure in Comfort: Report by the Public Protector on an investigation into allegations of impropriety and unethi-cal conduct relating to the installation and implementation of security measures by the Department of Public Works at and in respect of the pri-vate residence of President Jacob Zuma at Nkandla in the KwaZulu-Natal province', Report No: 25 of 2013/24, 19 March 2014, p 39. Available at www.gov.za/sites/www.gov.za/files/Public%20Protector%27s%20Report%20on%20Nkandla_a.pdf, accessed on 15 September 2017.
4    Ibid, p 56.

5    Ibid, p 57.

6    Ibid, p 63.

7    Ibid, p 68.

8    Constitutional Court of South Africa, judgment, *Economic Freedom Fighters* v *Speaker of the National Assembly and Others*; *Democratic Alliance* v *Speaker of the National Assembly and Others* [2016] ZACC 11, Cases CCT 143/15 and CCT 171/15, 31 March 2016, p 4. Available at www.corruptionwatch.org.za/download-constitutional-court-nkandla-judgment/, accessed on 15 September 2017.

9    Ibid, p 13.

10   Ibid, p 27.

11   Ibid, p 48.

12   Ibid, p 51.

13   Ibid, p 52.

14   Gareth van Onselen, 'Zuma versus Gordhan: A quotes timeline', *Business Day*, 29 March 2017.

15   Ibid.

16   Ibid.

17   Ibid.

18   Ibid.

19   Ibid.

20   Ibid.

21   Ibid.

22   Ibid.

23   Ibid.

24   Ibid.

25   Liesl Peyper, 'Ramaphosa offers "moral and political support" to Gordhan', News24, 16 October 2016. Available at www.news24.com/SouthAfrica/News/ramaphosa-offers-moral-and-political-support-to-gordhan-20161016, accessed on 15 September 2017.

26   Ibid.

27   Mzilikazi wa Afrika, 'Ajay Gupta "offered millions" to Jonas to "work with us"', *Sunday Times*, 23 October 2016.

28   Chris Yelland, 'Analysis: How much will new nuclear electricity cost South Africa?', *Daily Maverick*, 2 August 2016. Available at www.dailymaverick.co.za/article/2016-08-02-analysis-how-much-will-new-nuclear-electricity-cost-south-africa, accessed on 2 October 2016.

29   Mpho Raborife, 'I did report on Gupta "bullying", says Maseko', *Sowetan*, 23 March 2016. Available at www.sowetanlive.co.za/news/2016/03/23/i-did-report-gupta-bullying-says-maseko, accessed on 2 October 2017.

30   Pieter-Louis Myburgh, *The Republic of Gupta: A Story of State Capture* (Penguin, 2017), p 200.
31   Ibid.
32   Ray Hartley, 'NPA head Shaun Abrahams announces Gordhan decision', *Rand Daily Mail*, 31 October 2016.
33   Constitution of the Republic of South Africa Act 108 of 1996, section 89(1).
34   Peyper, 'Ramaphosa offers "moral and political support" to Gordhan'.
35   Van Onselen, 'Zuma versus Gordhan'.
36   All quotations from the memorial service are taken from the author's notes.
37   Masego Rahlaga, 'Ramaphosa says he is firmly opposed to Gordhan's removal', EWN, 31 March 2017. Available at ewn.co.za/2017/03/31/ramaphosa-opposes-gordhan-s-removal, accessed on 14 October 2017.
38   Ibid.

### Chapter 9: **To the front line**

1    Katherine Child, 'Twitterati fight back against fake pro-Gupta Twitter bots', TimesLIVE, 9 July 2017. Available at www.timeslive.co.za/politics/2017-07-09-twitterati-fight-back-against-fake-pro-gupta-twitter-bots/, accessed on 2 October 2017.
2    The articles are available at www.businesslive.co.za/authors/lily-gosam/.
3    Public Protector South Africa, 'State of Capture', Report no: 6 of 2016/17, 2 November 2016. Available at www.pprotect.org/library/investigation_report/2016-17/State_Capture_14October2016.pdf, accessed on 2 October 2017.
4    Ibid, p 3.
5    'Statement by Deputy Minister of Finance Mr Mcebisi Jonas (MP)', media statement, 16 March 2016. Available at www.treasury.gov.za/comm_media/press/2016/2016031601%20-%20Statement%20by%20Deputy%20Minister%20Jonas.pdf, accessed on 18 September 2017.
6    Public Protector South Africa, 'State of Capture', pp 5–7.
7    Ibid, pp 14–15.
8    Ibid, p 20.
9    Ibid, p 21.
10   Ibid, p 301.
11   Ibid, pp 353–354.
12   State Capacity Research Project (Mark Swilling, Convenor), 'Betrayal of the Promise: How South Africa Is Being Stolen', May 2017, p 4. Available at pari.org.za/wp-content/uploads/2017/05/Betrayal-of-the-Promise-25052017.pdf, accessed on 18 September 2017.

13  Ibid.

14  Ibid.

15  Ibid, p 6.

16  #Siyavuma Cyril Ramaphosa 2017, No 8, 14 July 2017. Available at ramaphosa.org.za/wp-content/uploads/2017/07/newsletter_8.pdf, accessed on 18 September 2017.

17  Ibid.

18  Joel Netshitenze, 'Monopoly capital is a global one, in SA it's mainly white dominated: Joel Netshitenzhe', SABC Digital News, 4 July 2017. Available at www.youtube.com/watch?v=ReDOQ8aMSKk, accessed on 14 October 2017.

19  'Cyril Ramaphosa: What needs to be done about the Guptas', Rand Daily Mail, 13 July 2017. Available at www.businesslive.co.za/rdm/politics/2017-07-13-cyril-ramaphosa-what-needs-to-be-done-about-the-guptas/, accessed on 18 September 2017.

20  Ibid.

21  Ibid.

22  Ibid.

23  Govan Whittles, 'Why Cosatu believes Ramaphosa will save the ANC', Mail & Guardian, 24 November 2016.

24  African News Agency, '"Ramaphosa meets our criteria for president: Cosatu"', Polity, 24 November 2016. Available at www.polity.org.za/article/ramaphosa-meets-our-criteria-for-president-cosatu-2016-11-24, accessed on 18 September 2017.

25  Ibid.

26  Cyril Ramaphosa, 'Ramaphosa addresses COSATU CEC meeting', ANN7, 30 May 2017. Available at www.youtube.com/watch?v=FGG7FeYgnw0, accessed on 14 October 2017.

27  Paul Herman, 'Sanco endorses Ramaphosa for ANC president', News24, 13 May 2017. Available at www.news24.com/SouthAfrica/News/sanco-endorses-ramaphosa-for-anc-president-20170513, accessed on 18 September 2017.

28  Hlengiwe Nhlabathi, 'Mashatile endorses Ramaphosa', News24, 18 June 2017. Available at www.news24.com/SouthAfrica/News/mashatile-endorses-ramaphosa-20170617, accessed on 18 September 2017.

29  'Cyril Ramaphosa: What needs to be done about the Guptas'.

30  Sibongile Mashaba, 'Outrage over Bathabile Dlamini's revelations', Sowetan, 14 August 2017. Available at www.sowetanlive.co.za/news/2017/

08/14/outrage-over-bathabile-dlamini-s-revelations, accessed on 19 September 2017.

31 Staff Reporter, 'Mboweni speaks out on "dirty tricks" against Ramaphosa', *Rand Daily Mail*, 16 August 2017. Available at www.businesslive.co.za/rdm/politics/2017-08-16-mboweni-speaks-out-on-dirty-tricks-against-ramaphosa/, accessed on 19 September 2017.

32 Ibid.

33 #Siyavuma Cyril Ramaphosa 2017, 'Dirty tricks won't derail efforts of CR17', Facebook post, 14 August 2017. Available at www.facebook.com/CR17SIYAVUMA/posts/890634261100389, accessed on 14 October 2017.

34 Stephen Grootes, '"Cyril would not beat up a woman', Eyewitness News, 16 August 2017. Available at ewn.co.za/2017/08/16/cyril-would-not-beat-up-a-woman, accessed on 19 September 2017.

35 Steven Motale, Ramaphosa 'the player', Sunday Independent, 3 September 2017.

36 Mzilikazi wa Afrika, 'Ramaphosa speaks out: I'm not a blesser, but I did have an affair', *Sunday Times*, 3 September 2017.

37 Ibid.

38 Ibid.

39 Ibid.

## Chapter 10: **Turbulent ascent**

1 Unless otherwise stated, all quotations in this chapter are from the author's own notes.

2 Olebogeng Molatlhwa, 'Over 400 delegates won't be allowed to vote for new ANC leader', TimesLIVE, 17 December 2017. Available at www.timeslive.co.za/anc-conference-2017/2017-12-17-over-400-delegates-wont-be-allowed-to-vote-for-new-anc-leader/, accessed on 20 March 2018.

3 Natasha Marrian and Genevieve Quintal, 'Numbers game keeps shifting at ANC elective conference', *Business Day*, 18 December 2017. Available at www.businesslive.co.za/bd/politics/2017-12-18-numbers-game-keeps-shifting-at-anc-elective-conference/, accessed on 20 March 2018.

4 Eyewitness News, 'WATCH: Ramaphosa tackles issue of 68 disputed votes', 20 December 2017. Available at ewn.co.za/2017/12/20/watch-cyril-ramaphosa-tackles-issue-of-68-disputed-votes, accessed on 20 March 2018.

### Chapter 11: **Twelve days in February**

1   Bloomberg Television, 'Ramaphosa calls corruption fight a mammoth task', YouTube, 24 January 2018. Available at www.youtube.com/watch?v= VgisIH8M6R4, accessed on 20 March 2018.

2   Ray Hartley, 'ANC in transition: a movement caught between old and new', *Business Day*, 16 February 2018. Available at www.businesslive. co.za/bd/politics/2018-02-16-anc-in-transition-a-movement-caught-between-old-and-new/, accessed on 7 April 2018.

3   Ibid.

4   Lindsay Dentlinger, 'Mashatile: President Zuma must go now', Eyewitness News, 14 February 2018. Available at ewn.co.za/2018/02/14/mashatile-president-zuma-must-go-now, accessed on 7 April 2018.

5   News24 Video, 'WATCH: President responds to NEC recall', 14 February 2018. Available at www.news24.com/Video/SouthAfrica/News/watch-live-president-zuma-addresses-nation-on-anc-recall-20180214, accessed on 20 March 2018.

6   Ibid.

7   Ibid.

8   Eyewitness News, '[MUST READ] Jacob Zuma's resignation address', 14 February 2018. Available at ewn.co.za/2018/02/15/must-read-jacob-zuma-s-resignation-address, accessed on 20 March 2018.

9   Ibid.

10  SABC Digital News, 'Cyril Ramaphosa sworn in as RSA president', YouTube, 15 February 2018. Available at www.youtube.com/watch?v=ttJK91DdPWk, accessed on 7 April 2018.

11  TimesLive, '[IN FULL] Read Cyril Ramaphosa's first state of the nation address', 16 February 2018. Available at www.timeslive.co.za/politics/ 2018-02-16-in-full--read-cyril-ramaphosas-first-state-of-the-nation-address/, accessed on 20 March 2018.

12  Jan Gerber, 'National Assembly adopts motion of land expropriation without compensation', News24, 27 February 2018. Available at www.news24. com/SouthAfrica/News/breaking-national-assembly-adopts-motion-on-land-expropriation-without-compensation-20180227, accessed on 20 March 2018.

13  Eyewitness News, 'President Ramaphosa's new Cabinet', 26 February 2018. Available at ewn.co.za/2018/02/26/watch-live-ramaphosa-reshuffles-his-cabinet, accessed on 20 March 2018.

## Postscript

1   TimesLive, '[IN FULL] Read Cyril Ramaphosa's first state of the nation address', 16 February 2018. Available at www.timeslive.co.za/politics/2018-02-16-in-full--read-cyril-ramaphosas-first-state-of-the-nation-address/, accessed on 20 March 2018.

2   Ibid.

# Index

Page numbers in *italics* refer to photographs.